# LUMINARY
## BAKERY

*Rising Hope*

# LUMINARY
## BAKERY

# Rising Hope

# Recipes and Stories from Luminary Bakery

Rachel Stonehouse and Kaila H. Johnson

With Alice Williams and Rachael Coulson

## HARPER
## DESIGN
*An Imprint of HarperCollinsPublishers*

# CONTENTS

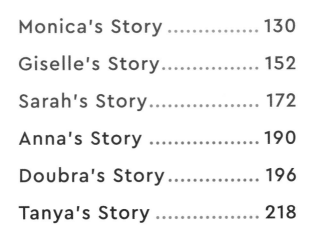

# INTRODUCTION

BY ALICE WILLIAMS,
FOUNDER OF LUMINARY BAKERY

If you were to walk into a Luminary Bakery on an ordinary day, you would be met with the smell of freshly baked cinnamon swirls and a warm greeting from one of our café team. You would see a mix of locals gathering for a quiet coffee or holding a meeting, the hustle and bustle of cakes being decorated, and you might see several women coming in and being greeted like family.

Luminary is a London-based bakery on a mission to empower some of the UK's most disadvantaged women. In this book, you are invited behind the scenes, to learn our treasured recipes and hear the stories of hope that rise behind our bakery doors.

Over the years, we have often been asked to write a recipe book, with loyal customers longing to know the secret to our cinnamon swirls or fluffy focaccia. And many of the women we have supported through baking have been keen to share their life stories, to encourage others to find hope in any circumstances. We have met so many courageous women, and working with them to create this book has given us all the opportunity to reflect on how far we have come as individuals, as well as collectively.

Meeting women who were experiencing extreme poverty, disadvantage, and violence was the inspiration for starting Luminary. There was one encounter in particular that stands out in my mind ...

I remember where I was when I met her, standing on Vallance Road near Whitechapel at one o'clock in the morning, with the City of London skyline behind us. I was volunteering with a local charity, Door of Hope, taking out necessary supplies to women working in the red-light area. She was cold, fed up, and not making enough money. When I asked if there were any other ways for her to earn an income, she replied, "I don't know how to do anything else, I've been doing this since I was thirteen."

I met many women like her and not just those "street-working"; I also volunteered in a homeless hostel, many of whose female residents had experienced abuse and were living in poverty. The world of skyscrapers, wealth, high-end restaurants, and coffee chains—just a stone's throw away from where they were living—could have been a million miles away for the lack of opportunities it offered them. All had lived through harrowing things and yet they were survivors, fighters, hustlers, mothers, defenders— these women had potential. I couldn't stand by and see it go to waste. I couldn't bear to see them struggling to get by every day, questioning their value, and unable to provide a different future for their children.

Although we didn't have much, our small team from a local church (Kahaila on Brick Lane, London) decided to set about changing the landscape for these local women forever. Abigail Mifsud (a food blogger and home baker), Sarah Harrison (a home baker and a volunteer chef in the homeless hostel), and I decided to use the skills our team had and began to teach the women we met how to bake.

Initially, this was just for women in the homeless hostel, which was a great setting for us to start getting to know local women. Each of them had a different journey that had led them there: some had fled a violent partner; some had left prison and had nowhere to go; some had been rough sleeping and this was finally a place to call home. Some of the women were already great cooks and some had never tried baking before, but they all wanted the opportunity to do something creative, something for themselves, and something they could share with others. Their skills began to improve and we spent time investing in them as individuals, in their personal growth, overcoming trauma, and preparing to build a career in the food industry.

And hope began to rise.

Another local church generously gave us space in their kitchen to bake products to sell at Kahaila Café, and we took samples to other local companies. Our little business gained momentum and we secured a contract with Ben & Jerry's to provide all the baked goods for their first UK store. We soon outgrew the church kitchen and had the opportunity to move into a larger kitchen nearby. Here, we brought in even more women to train.

The first day of our training course is always nerve-racking for trainees as they take the brave step to enter a new

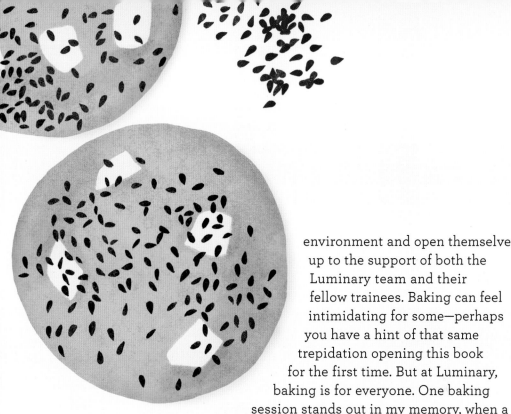

environment and open themselves up to the support of both the Luminary team and their fellow trainees. Baking can feel intimidating for some—perhaps you have a hint of that same trepidation opening this book for the first time. But at Luminary, baking is for everyone. One baking session stands out in my memory, when a woman who struggled with her concentration and comprehension of theory eventually saw her loaf of bread come out of the oven. She burst into tears and exclaimed, "I can't have made that! It's so perfect!" When we finally convinced her that it was in fact her loaf, her confidence soared.

We start with the basics, as our trainees venture into the world of baking and begin to understand the importance of thoroughly reading a recipe before enthusiastically launching in. Then, we gradually build on their accomplishments, challenging them with more technical bakes as their skills and confidence grow. You are welcome to take a similar approach, challenging yourself to try a new product weekly, as our women do, or simply dip into the book to try out a new recipe when you fancy, or have an occasion to bake for.

The support we offer women at Luminary is not just centered around baking—we also want women to learn, to dream, and to share with one another. Seeing them start to take brave steps in opening up is magical. As Brené Brown says, "We can't be brave in the big world without at least one small safe space to work through our fears and falls." This is the space Luminary has always sought to be. There is no judgment here—about your past, present, or your future.

As Luminary has grown, we have built strong partnerships with organizations who support women with traumatic life experiences. They might have survived human trafficking, domestic abuse, the criminal justice system, or leaving care. Often, the common factors that they have each lived through are poverty, homelessness, and mental health issues as a result of the trauma they have endured. Some services classify women who have experienced this type of multiple disadvantage as "vulnerable" adults, and while it is important to recognize where people need extra support, in our experience women shouldn't necessarily be labeled as vulnerable. After all, it is their strength and resilience that has got them to where they are today. At Luminary, we have moved toward the word "disadvantaged." This makes it clear that the women's life experiences are down to their situation, and not a comment on their strength of character.

One of our favorite moments every year is the graduation ceremony that we hold to celebrate our women completing the full six-month program. At this, they display their showstopping cakes and we present them with their certificates. Our first group of trainees graduated in March 2015, at one of the most powerful and emotional evenings I've ever experienced. They invited friends and family, showcased their impressive bakes, shared a little of their stories, and we celebrated them. They deserved it. These women, and the many others who have graduated since—the women in this book—are now making their way in the world, building their careers, and inspiring us every day.

Luminary Bakery found its very own home in 2016, on Allen Road in Stoke Newington, London, after two years of baking in generous kitchens nearby. It had always been our dream to move from wholesale production to opening our doors to the public, creating more job opportunities for the women we train. And with the help of significant grants and a crowdfunding campaign to buy equipment, this vision became a reality. Our fourth cohort started their training the day after we moved in; needless to say, it was chaos!

But we soon found our feet, and those women were so excited to be the first to benefit from the new space.

Over the last few years, Luminary has gone from strength to strength—growing our social enterprise into something sustainable, opening a second location in Camden in London, training nearly 100 women, tackling huge orders with a small team, and getting to the point where we were even making cakes for the Duchess of Sussex! All the while, we have journeyed with our women through starting their careers, building their own businesses, moving house, getting married, overcoming their fears, navigating the complicated transition from welfare to work, raising children, and even being by their side during childbirth.

This is the Luminary family.

Too often, violence and trauma isolate us from community, when that is the very thing we need the most. We want to thank every woman who has joined Luminary, because it takes courage to step into the bakery on that first day. We hope that they have felt welcomed, accepted, loved, and inspired, and we know that they have helped create that safe haven for others, too. These women are why Luminary exists, and they make it an exciting, uplifting, and vibrant community to be a part of. This book is a chance for them—and for others who have been involved—to share some of their stories with you, along with their favorite recipes.

This is a book bursting with hope—filled with the stories of women who held on to hope when they thought all was lost. Each narrative is uniquely powerful, but together they remind us that strength comes in community.

Every woman has shown immense courage to survive her circumstances alone, but it is only when she is embraced by others that she can really start to fulfill her potential. There are caring friends, compassionate doctors, and proactive support workers who have all given these women the confidence to take brave steps in their lives and careers.

Baking is special and it connects people in a way that is difficult to describe. Baking together bridges cultures, social classes, and differing life experiences. Baking can raise hope in people who had forgotten their own potential, their power.

Our dream for this book is that it inspires you to raise hope in your community, too. Maybe you will bake one of these recipes to share with someone who is going through a tough time. Perhaps you will be as brave as the women in this book to share with others your journey of overcoming adversity. You might challenge a friend to bake through the book with you and go on a journey of discovering your potential. Whatever way this inspires you, we thank you for joining in with the hope that is rising at Luminary.

# HALIMOT'S STORY

Halimot's story truly represents the rising hope that is always within us, even in the darkest of times, and we're so proud to call her one of Luminary's graduates.

At a young age, Halimot was trafficked into modern slavery by someone she trusted. Although she eventually escaped after several years of being held against her will, the trauma of her experience dramatically impacted her day-to-day living. Years later, after overcoming so much and starting a family, she continued to keep her past a secret out of concern for her children and worry that the traffickers would find her again.

It wasn't until Halimot's depression spiraled out of control that she finally opened up to her doctor about her past. This was the moment when things began to change. She was introduced to a charity that worked with women from trafficked backgrounds, offering support and counseling. It was then that the charity introduced her to Alice and Luminary Bakery.

*"I didn't trust people at all—I lost trust completely—but I thought I'd give Luminary a chance. On the first day, sharing it with people who understood my background, I knew I was going to do it! The care I received from the ladies at Luminary brought up so many emotions. Someone even offered me a drink! It had been a long time since someone cared for me like that."*

At the start, each day was a challenge to overcome, as things didn't always work out as she wanted them to. But, unlike before, she had people to fall back on and Halimot found the encouragement she received from Luminary therapeutic. As she began to grow in her knowledge of baking, each day became a success. Not only did Halimot graduate from our program, but she went on to start her own business (see page 255).

Halimot's love of food and of bringing people together has grown into an innate desire to create community, whether at her children's school, in her neighborhood, or at Luminary events. Her former life, where isolation became the only option, has slowly transitioned into a life with rising hope in others, full of encouragement, strength, and love for people.

*"Whenever people say that my baking tastes good, it heals me! I don't see my clients as simply people ordering from me, I see them as helping me process and heal."*

Halimot continues to bring a warmth to Luminary that impacts each new group of trainees. Together, she has been part of helping us build a family of warriors and overcomers, leaning on and encouraging each other, and empowering each woman that comes through our doors to reach their potential. We are a family! Through celebrations, heartache, business challenges, and the ups and downs of life, we work through it all together. Halimot's wisdom, advice, and encouragement never cease to amaze us—she is an incredibly gifted woman.

*"Never give up! What has happened in the past has happened. You cannot change the clock. Don't give up, but change it in a positive way. There's no going back to yesterday. There's only moving forward to tomorrow!"*

Now, *that* is rising hope.

# EQUIPMENT & BAKING NOTES

We recognize that no one has everything—whether that's specific tools, access to certain ingredients, financial resources, or even time; we're all short of something! With this in mind, we've included bakes that cover a range of different options. There are recipes for when you're short of time (which take about 30 minutes to make); economical recipes (cheap to make or which make use of food that would normally be thrown away); and recipes for those with special dietary requirements (vegan, gluten-free, and lactose-free). The Special Indexes section on page 250 will help you find them.

**Measurements:** As bakers, we're passionate about precise measurements and weighing out ingredients accurately. A recipe is a specific set of instructions and, if followed faithfully, should produce consistent results the way the author intended. Unlike soup, where a few extra vegetables, broth, or seasoning could go undetected, where baking is concerned even a little deviation from the recipe can have a big effect!

We find using weight to measure ingredients (rather than volume measurements) produces more consistent products. For this reason, in our bakery we always use an electronic food scale to measure ingredients. We weigh everything from salt to flour, bananas to oil.

An electronic scale is more accurate than a mechanical one because it is more sensitive, allowing us to measure small incremental amounts of ingredients as well as liquids straight into our mixing bowls.

You only need to become familiar with the "tare" function on an electronic scale, which will bring the read-out back to zero after you have placed your bowl on the scale. This saves on cleaning up (always a bonus), but is also far easier and quicker than trying to judge the level of water in a measuring cup or to guestimate ¼ ounce of salt, for instance. Fruit, vegetables, and herbs also vary in size depending on the variety and supplier, so for these too we give a weight in ounces to ensure a consistent bake.

We have given liquid quantities in fluid ounces, because if you have an electronic scale that also weighs fluid ounces, it's much more accurate to measure liquids by weight, rather than doing it by eye. Wonderfully, 1 fluid ounce of water weighs 1 ounce, so it's an easy conversion. However, if your scale does not weigh fluid ounces, check your conversions.

Similarly, for baking, don't use any old household teaspoons and tablespoons to measure out your ingredients, as they can vary in size. Instead, use a set of measuring spoons. All teaspoon and tablespoon measurements are level unless stated otherwise.
1 teaspoon = 5ml
1 tablespoon = 15ml

**Ovens:** Just like people, every oven has a different temperament, running at different temperatures to what they're supposed to be programed to. This can sadly result in over- or undercooked bakes and be so disappointing if you've just invested time and money into creating a recipe. If you bake regularly, you hopefully have a good grasp on whether (and if so, where) your oven has hotspots and whether it bakes hotter or cooler than other ovens. We advise you to adjust the temperatures in the recipes slightly to account for this and also rotate products within the oven to help bake them evenly. If you're new to your oven, we recommend using an oven thermometer, which will reveal the true temperature of your oven. You can then adjust the oven dial to achieve the temperature required in each recipe.

**Scale:** As we've just mentioned, if you bake regularly and have the means to invest in an electronic (digital) scale, we can't recommend it enough—it will transform your baking! But if not, don't fear—we've made sure all the recipes in this book can be made with whatever equipment you have, and smaller precise measurements (such as ¼ ounce of salt) are also given in teaspoons for ease.

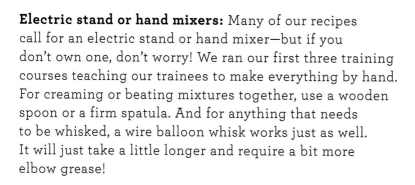

**Electric stand or hand mixers:** Many of our recipes call for an electric stand or hand mixer—but if you don't own one, don't worry! We ran our first three training courses teaching our trainees to make everything by hand. For creaming or beating mixtures together, use a wooden spoon or a firm spatula. And for anything that needs to be whisked, a wire balloon whisk works just as well. It will just take a little longer and require a bit more elbow grease!

**Bench scrapers:** Lots of bakers use a simple piece of equipment called a "bench scraper" for making bread or decorating cakes. It's a rectangle of plastic or metal, usually with one curved and one straight edge, used to divide doughs, scrape them off counters, and help knead. When kneading bread, it can be tempting to dust the counter you're using with flour to stop the dough sticking, but this can result in a dryer, harder bread, because you end up mixing all that extra flour into the dough. Instead, fearlessly let the dough stick to the counter and use a bench scraper to scrape off any that's stuck, bringing it back into the ball of dough. A bench scraper can also be used as a cake scraper, to evenly smooth frosting over the surface of a layer cake. If you're making lots of bread, particularly very wet doughs such as focaccia, you might find investing a few dollars in one makes a world of difference.

**Cake decorating tools:** At Luminary, we use a few bits of equipment only keen cake makers usually own, such

as a turntable, palette knife, and cake scraper. They make getting a perfectly smooth finish on a cake a lot easier and are well worth the investment if you decorate cakes regularly. If you don't have these to hand, you can place the cake on a large, flat plate and rotate it on your counter instead of using a turntable. And a butter knife and spatula are enough in place of a palette knife or cake scraper.

**Silicone spatula:** We always have a silicone spatula on hand, for getting every last bit of mixture out of the bowl or pan.

**Pastry brush:** You'll find a pastry brush very useful for glazing and greasing, too.

**Baking parchment and silicone baking mats/pan liners:** There is sometimes confusion over whether to use baking parchment or wax paper. Wax paper is better reserved for sandwich wrapping as a lot of baked goods will stick like glue to it. If you're standing perplexed in the grocery store, buy "baking parchment," which is the better option. For baking cookies, silicone baking mats can be a useful and sustainable purchase to replace baking parchment, as they can be washed up and reused many times. You can now also buy reusable silicone cake pan liners.

# BREAD

There is something inviting about the smell of freshly baked bread. The delicious warm fragrance brings to mind moments, whether dreamed or experienced, of the comforts of home, when families gather and food is shared. In our Luminary cafés, the aromas from the bakery fill each room, awakening nostalgia and the anticipation of flavors before you get the chance to satisfy your mouthwatering cravings.

Through learning to make our signature cinnamon swirls and fluffy focaccia, Luminary trainees have found breadmaking to be therapeutic—it brings a moment of peace in weeks that can sometimes feel chaotic. Physically kneading the dough can help release outside frustrations and give space for mental freewheeling; likewise, the rhythmic process can absorb your attention and help you to be present in the task. For this meditative activity to result in something our trainees are proud to feed their families, we believe there is something remarkably nourishing about bread.

# TINA'S STORY

On special occasions, we gather our loved ones together to honor specific moments in time and share delicious food. For Tina, one of our trainees, the memory of Easter in her Polish homeland brought such a picture of happy times to mind.

In Poland, Easter is family focused, full of traditions and collective preparations for the day ahead. For Tina, the centerpiece of it all was *chałka* bread—a Jewish braided enriched loaf, full of rich, buttery flavors. According to tradition, once the *chałka* dough had been blessed by the church, everyone had to dance for the time it was baking in the oven. If you sat down at any point, the fear was that the *chałka* would also sit and go flat! With dance and laughter filling the kitchen, the dough would "come alive!"

What makes this bread so special is the fact that it is enjoyed only once a year. It was a time that Tina looked forward to and a memory that still fills her with joy.

> *"I was six years old when I first experienced* chałka. *I was at home with my mom, dad, sister, and brother. It was magical: the smell, the dancing, and laughter."*

But life isn't always so magical. Years later, Tina found herself homeless when her landlord ended her contract so that he could upgrade the living space. With no place to go and no financially viable options, Tina began to live on the streets of London. After five months with no safe shelter, yet not a priority for public housing, she found a homeless hostel for temporary refuge. Life was bleak and she began to believe that there was no way out. It wasn't until she saw an advertisement for a baking course with Luminary that things started to turn around.

Tina didn't start our program with the kind of confidence needed to experiment with baking methods and flavors. Prior to starting, she described herself as anxious and hesitant. But as the course progressed and her knowledge of baking grew, so did her creativity and excitement to explore. This newfound confidence brought us the recipes she contributed to this book.

One of the modules taught on the course is breadmaking. Tina thought it was going to be difficult, but found it came naturally to her. It had such an impact that, after graduation, she went on to train at a London bread bakery, refining her skills and mastering her knowledge and understanding of this everyday staple.

To this day, Tina returns to Luminary to teach bread lessons to our trainees. This honor of returning as a teacher to where she was once a trainee is an experience she finds powerful and a process we find to be fully restorative.

*"Luminary is a provider in so many ways. They have fed my body, spirit, dreams, and imagination as to what's possible in the future. I'm certainly a different person— I'm brand-new!"*

# TINA'S
# Chalka Bread

Dust off your Polish mazurka costume and gather your friends and family. This loaf of bread is the perfect focal point for discovering sweet, lively memories. Tina has put her own spin on this Easter recipe—you can enjoy it at any time of the year!

**MAKES 1 MEDIUM LOAF**

**For the loaf**
2 fluid ounces whole milk
1¾ ounces superfine sugar
2 ounces unsalted butter, softened
¼ teaspoon fine salt

1 x ¼-ounce packet of active dry yeast
¼ teaspoon vanilla extract
1 large egg, beaten
6 ounces white bread flour, plus extra for dusting
1½ ounces raisins or golden raisins

1 tablespoon vegetable or sunflower oil, for greasing

**For the crumble topping (optional)**
1 ounce cold butter, cubed
1½ ounces all-purpose flour
4 teaspoons superfine sugar

Warm the milk in a large pan over low heat until lukewarm (about the same temperature as your finger), but don't let it boil. Remove the pan from the heat, then stir in the sugar, softened butter, and salt.

In a small bowl, mix the dried yeast with 1 tablespoon warm water, then pour the mixture into the milk mixture, along with the vanilla and half of the beaten egg and whisk together. There might still be some small lumps of butter—this is okay.

Add 3½ ounces of the flour to the mixture and beat with a wooden spoon until completely smooth with no floury lumps. Stir in the remaining flour and raisins.

Tip the sticky dough out onto a lightly floured counter and knead for 5 to 10 minutes until smooth and elastic. Alternatively, you can use an electric mixer fitted with a dough hook to do all the messy kneading for you. You'll be able to tell when it's ready by holding a little piece of dough up to a light or window and stretching it between your fingers. If you can stretch the dough thin enough that

you can see the light through it without it tearing, it's done! This is called the "windowpane test."

Grease a large bowl with the oil and tip the dough into it, turning to coat it in the oil. Cover the bowl with a damp dish towel or plastic wrap and leave in a warm place for 60 to 90 minutes until the dough is doubled in size.

Punch the dough back down inside the bowl, then divide into 3 equal pieces. Roll each piece of dough into a long sausage, about 12 inches long and ¾ inch wide. Join the strands of dough together at one end with a dab of beaten egg and braid them. At this point, you can either leave it as one long braid or spiral it into a round loaf shape. Transfer it to a baking sheet lined with baking parchment, cover, and leave in a warm place for 60 to 90 minutes until doubled in size.

Meanwhile, preheat the oven to 400°F.

If making the crumble topping, rub the butter into the flour until it looks like bread crumbs, then stir through the sugar. With a pastry brush (or your fingers), brush the top of the loaf with the remaining beaten egg and sprinkle the crumble across the top.

Bake in the oven for 25 to 30 minutes until golden brown. (Dancing in the kitchen while it's baking isn't mandatory, but it's a laugh!)

Let cool and enjoy sliced with butter, jam, or on its own.

---

### TIP

Lots of bakers use a simple piece of equipment called a "bench scraper" to help make bread. It's a rectangle of plastic or metal, usually with one curved and one straight edge, used to divide doughs, scrape them off counters, and help knead. If you're making lots of bread, particularly very wet doughs such as focaccia, you might find investing in one makes a world of difference.

---

# Buttered New Potato and Garden Herb Focaccia

When it comes to baking different breads, the stickier your dough is, the softer the finished product will be. For those willing to embrace the mess, the reward of our beautifully soft and pillowy focaccia is well worth getting your hands completely covered in dough for!

**MAKES 1 LARGE LOAF (6 TO 8 LARGE SQUARES)**

**For the dough**

19¾ ounces white bread flour

2 teaspoons salt

2½ x ¼-ounce packets of active dry yeast

2 tablespoons olive oil, plus extra for greasing

**For the topping**

10½ ounces new potatoes

1¾ ounces unsalted butter, melted (substitute dairy-free spread if you want to make this vegan)

3½ tablespoons olive oil

A few fresh rosemary stalks (about ¼ ounce), picked into small sprigs

A few fresh thyme sprigs (about ⅛ ounce), with any woody stems removed

A small handful of fresh sage (about ¼ ounce), leaves picked and coarsely chopped

3 tablespoons fresh or dried oregano (about ⅛ ounce)

1 tablespoon kosher or sea salt

Weigh the flour into a large mixing bowl. Add the salt to one side of the bowl and the yeast to the other, making sure they don't touch (if the yeast comes into direct contact with the salt it can retard it and stop your focaccia from rising). Toss the salt in some of the flour surrounding it and do the same with the yeast, finally mixing it all together until combined.

Make a well in the middle of the flour and pour in 15¼ fluid ounces warm water and the olive oil. Using a bench scraper or wooden spoon, mix the liquids into the flour until a sloppy dough forms and there are no lumps of flour left.

Oil your hands with a little olive oil and tip the wet dough out onto a clean counter. Knead for 10 to 15 minutes, stopping to scrape down the counter every few minutes and bringing it back together. Don't be afraid of how sticky it is—avoid the temptation to add extra flour to the table, your hands, or the dough. Alternatively, you can use an electric mixer fitted with a dough hook to do all the messy kneading for you.

After kneading, the dough should be more supple and should hold itself together. Transfer it to an oiled bowl, cover with a damp dish towel or plastic wrap, and place somewhere warm for about 1 hour until it has doubled in size.

Once the dough has doubled in size, line a 9 x 13-inch baking pan with baking parchment and rub a tablespoon of oil over the pan and your hands. Push the risen dough down, knocking it back inside the bowl, before scraping and tipping it into the lined pan.

Roll the dough around inside the oiled pan so it's glistening with oil, then take the edges of the dough and gently pull, push, and wobble it into the corners of the baking pan without tearing it. Fold all the edges of the dough into the middle and turn it upside down to hide all the ugly bits and give you a nice supple, stretched top. Cover the pan with a dish towel/plastic wrap and leave in a warm place once again for 1 hour.

While you're waiting for the dough to rise this second time, slice the new potatoes into ¼-inch slices and mix with the melted butter, oil, and herbs.

When the dough is ready, push your fingers deep into the dough a few times, almost to the bottom of the pan, to create little dimples. Sprinkle the oily potato and herb topping over the top of the dough, followed by the kosher or sea salt. Let proof in a warm place for a final 15 minutes.

Meanwhile, preheat the oven to 425°F.

When the oven is hot, bake the focaccia for 20 to 25 minutes until golden brown and puffy.

Let cool a little before cutting into squares. This bread makes a mean sandwich or is a great accompaniment to meats and cheeses. Our café makes toasties from it every day, slicing the large squares in half and stuffing them with tasty fillings.

# MIMI'S
# Goat Cheese and Grape Focaccia

The joy of focaccia is all the space it gives for toppings! It's a blank canvas, waiting to be topped with whatever delicious ingredients take your fancy. Our bakers make fresh focaccia every day, creatively choosing toppings and regularly coming up with new seasonal flavors.

Mimi, one of our bakers, bounded into Luminary for her shift one day clutching a plastic bag brimming with jewel-like black grapes from the vines in her backyard, and they inspired the day's focaccia. We love how the grapes glisten and burst with sweet-sour juice as you bite into them, deliciously complementing the creamy goat cheese and heady olive oil.

**MAKES 1 LARGE LOAF (6 TO 8 LARGE PIECES)**

**For the dough**
17¾ ounces white bread flour
2 teaspoons salt
2½ x ¼-ounce packets of active dry yeast

2 tablespoons olive oil, plus extra for greasing

**For the topping**
9 ounces black seedless grapes
A handful of fresh rosemary (½ ounce), sprigs picked

3½ tablespoons olive oil
3½ ounces soft goat cheese, sliced into small chunks
1 tablespoon kosher or sea salt

Follow the same method for making the dough as for the focaccia on page 32, up until the dough is rising for a second time in its oiled baking pan.

Meanwhile, mix the grapes and rosemary in a bowl with the olive oil and set aside. Slice the goat cheese into ¾-inch pieces.

When the dough is ready, push your fingers deep into the dough a few times, almost to the bottom of the pan, to create little dimples. Sprinkle the grapes, rosemary, and oil across the top of the dough, followed by the goat cheese and kosher or sea salt. Let proof in a warm place for a final 15 minutes.

Meanwhile, preheat the oven to 425°F.

Bake the focaccia for 20 to 25 minutes until golden brown and puffy.

Let cool a little before cutting into squares. This is really good served alongside a cheese platter or cut into small squares as appetizers.

# TINA'S
# Chive-Marbled Rye Bread

When it comes to bread, Tina is Luminary's queen. Her fun-loving nature and ambitious dreaming are what brought together these delicious flavors. Rye bread was a part of her Polish upbringing, but she wanted to mix things up by adding a personal touch: "We always had chives in my family as there was an excess of them in the backyard! Not liking to see things go to waste, I decided to layer them into the bread mix and it turned out pretty swell!" This soft loaf with its beautiful, green swirls will bring a savory twist to any homecooked meal, and is especially good with chicken soup or borscht.

**MAKES 1 LOAF**

11 ounces white bread flour, plus extra for dusting

5½ ounces white rye flour

2½ teaspoons salt

1 x ¼-ounce packet active dry yeast

2 tablespoons vegetable or sunflower oil, plus a little extra for greasing

2 teaspoons blackstrap molasses

1½ ounces fresh chives, very finely chopped

Weigh the flours into a large bowl and add the salt to one side of the bowl and the yeast to the other, making sure they don't touch (see page 32). Toss the salt in the flour surrounding it, do the same with the yeast, and finally mix together until combined.

Make a well in the middle of the flour and pour in 10 fluid ounces warm water, the oil, and the blackstrap molasses. Mix until the mixture comes together but is still a messy clump and not yet a fully formed dough. Cover with a damp dish towel and let rest for 20 minutes.

Tip the half-formed dough onto a lightly floured counter and knead for about 10 minutes until it becomes elastic and stops sticking to the counter, regularly scraping down the counter with a bench scraper. Alternatively, use an electric mixer fitted with a dough hook to do all the messy kneading for you.

Divide the dough in half and knead the chives into one half until evenly distributed. Place the two doughs in separate oiled bowls, cover with a damp dish towel or plastic wrap, and leave in a warm place for about 1 hour, or until doubled in size.

Meanwhile, line the bottom of a 2-pound loaf pan with baking parchment and brush the sides with a little oil.

Turn the plain dough out onto a lightly floured counter and roll out into a rectangle, about 10 x 8 inches. Brush the surface of the dough with water. Roll the chive dough out to the same size and lay it on top of the plain dough, using the water as "glue" between them.

Take one of the short sides of dough and fold it over by ½ inch, then gently continue to roll the dough into a tight swirl, using your fingers and thumbs to work from one side to the other, rolling as tightly as possible. You should be left with a sausage of dough, about 8 inches long. Shape the dough into a loaf to fit the pan and tuck the ends under, then place it in the pan and cover with a damp dish towel or plastic wrap. Set aside in a warm place for 30 to 40 minutes until doubled in size again.

Meanwhile, preheat the oven to 450°F.

Slash the top of the risen loaf with a small sharp knife (Tina makes 5 diagonal cuts). Place it in the oven and immediately reduce the heat to 425°F. Bake for 40 to 45 minutes until it is golden brown and sounds hollow when taken out of the pan and tapped on the bottom.

Let cool completely before slicing. It's best eaten on the same day.

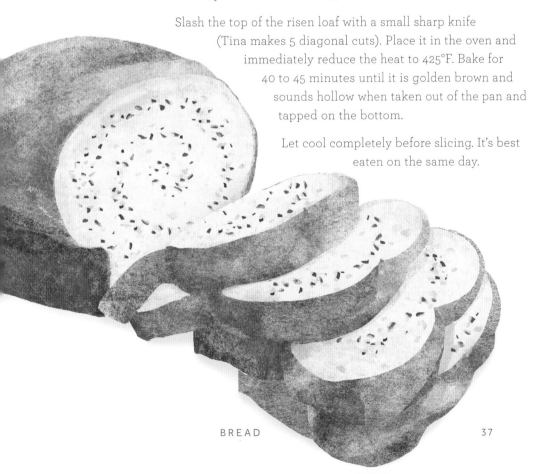

# Olive, Paprika, and Manchego Breadsticks

Our doughy batons are made for dipping and ripping, to be part of a tapas feast or served alongside fresh salads. Inspired by the flavors and colors of Spain, we're particularly fond of the way the paprika colors the dough to a warming red-orange hue and brings a smoky sweetness to the bread.

**MAKES 18 TO 20**

7 ounces all-purpose flour, plus extra for dusting

7 ounces white bread flour

1 tablespoon smoked paprika

2 teaspoons salt

1¼ teaspoons (⅛ ounce) active dry yeast

1 tablespoon olive oil, plus extra for greasing and brushing

3½ ounces black Kalamata olives, sliced (or any black olives are good)

1¾ ounces Manchego cheese, grated, plus extra for sprinkling

In a large bowl, mix together the two flours with the smoked paprika. Add the salt to one side of the bowl and the yeast to the other, making sure they don't touch. Toss the salt in some of the flour surrounding it and do the same with the yeast, finally mixing them all together until well combined. Make a well in the middle of the flour and pour in 8½ fluid ounces warm water and the olive oil. Mix together to form a sticky, messy dough.

Tip the dough out onto a clean counter and knead for about 10 minutes until smooth and supple.

Flatten out the dough, cover the surface with the sliced olives and grated cheese, then fold them into the dough. Knead until the olives and cheese are well dispersed throughout the dough.

Lightly grease the mixing bowl with a little oil, then put the ball of dough back into it and cover with a damp dish towel or plastic wrap.

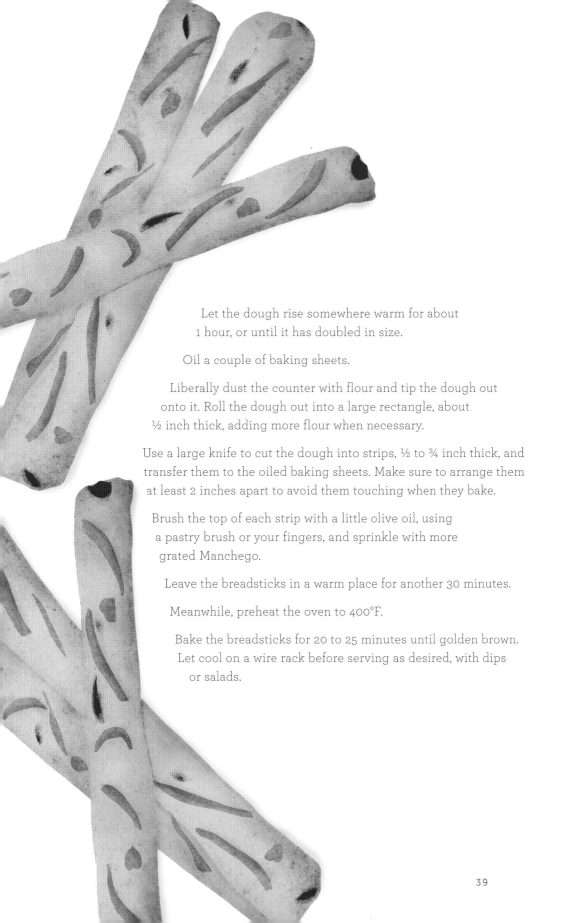

Let the dough rise somewhere warm for about
1 hour, or until it has doubled in size.

Oil a couple of baking sheets.

Liberally dust the counter with flour and tip the dough out
onto it. Roll the dough out into a large rectangle, about
½ inch thick, adding more flour when necessary.

Use a large knife to cut the dough into strips, ½ to ¾ inch thick, and
transfer them to the oiled baking sheets. Make sure to arrange them
at least 2 inches apart to avoid them touching when they bake.

Brush the top of each strip with a little olive oil, using
a pastry brush or your fingers, and sprinkle with more
grated Manchego.

Leave the breadsticks in a warm place for another 30 minutes.

Meanwhile, preheat the oven to 400°F.

Bake the breadsticks for 20 to 25 minutes until golden brown.
Let cool on a wire rack before serving as desired, with dips
or salads.

# OUR SIGNATURE
# English Muffins with Liz's Kumquat and Rosemary Marmalade

Our Liz is many things: an advocate, a leader, a whiz at business operations, a hospitality curator, and now a Luminary trustee. She arrived on the scene when Luminary was only a few months old and has been one of our biggest cheerleaders since. The combination of our English muffins with her Kumquat and Rosemary Marmalade (page 42) perfectly sums up how she makes our world that much sweeter.

**MAKES 12 MUFFINS**

7 fluid ounces buttermilk

1 tablespoon superfine sugar

1 x ¼-ounce packet of active dry yeast

1 ounce vegetable oil, plus extra for greasing

4 ounces unsalted butter, softened

18 ounces white bread flour

2 teaspoons salt

Fine cornmeal, for dusting

Heat 7 fluid ounces water and the buttermilk in a small pan until lukewarm (the same temperature as your finger and no hotter). Stir in the sugar and yeast and set aside for 10 minutes. After that time, stir in the oil and butter in chunks.

In a large bowl, mix the flour and salt. Make a well in the middle, add the liquids, and bring together into a sticky dough.

Knead the dough on a clean counter for 10 minutes, using a bench scraper to keep the counter clean and avoiding dusting it with additional flour (extra flour will give you hard and tough muffins). It'll be very sticky so try slapping it on the counter and folding it over repeatedly, to keep it from covering every inch of the surface. Alternatively, you can use an electric mixer fitted with a dough hook to do all the messy kneading for you.

Place the dough back into the bowl and cover with plastic wrap or a damp dish towel. Let it rise somewhere warm for 30 minutes. After this time, transfer the bowl to the refrigerator and let the dough rise for another 1 hour until it has doubled in size.

Line 2 large baking sheets with baking parchment and dust with a thin layer of cornmeal.

Oil your counter, tip the dough out onto it, and cut the dough into 12 equal pieces (about 3¼ ounces each). Flatten each piece into a 2-inch circle and fold the outside edges into the center, pinching them together. Turn the balls upside down (so the ugly pinched bit is on the bottom and the top is nice and smooth) and place on the baking sheets. Dust the muffin tops with a little extra cornmeal and loosely cover both sheets with oiled plastic wrap. Leave at room temperature for another 45 to 60 minutes until doubled in size.

Preheat the oven to 325°F, preheat a large skillet over low heat, and place a third, unlined baking sheet in the oven to heat up.

Carefully transfer 3 to 4 muffins upside down into the hot pan, using a couple of spatulas to lift them so that they maintain their shape. Cook for 10 minutes until they have golden brown bottoms, then flip each muffin and cook for another 5 to 6 minutes. Patience is everything here—let the muffins slowly brown and cook through or you'll have raw middles.

Transfer the cooked muffins to the baking sheet in the hot oven and bake for another 10 minutes. Once cooked, they'll spring back to the touch and feel light.

Let cool for 15 minutes before slicing open and serving with salted butter and your new favorite condiment ... (see page 42).

**TIP**
If you can't find buttermilk, you can substitute a mixture of 5 ounces yogurt and 2½ fluid ounces whole milk.

# LIZ'S
# Kumquat and Rosemary Marmalade

Essential for spreading on our English muffins (page 40), this is also brilliant on toast or spread between the layers of a sponge cake.

**MAKES 6 X 6-OUNCE JARS**

35 ounces kumquats
35 ounces superfine sugar
1 teaspoon finely chopped
   fresh rosemary

Slice the kumquats into ¼-inch circles, removing and setting aside any seeds. Place the seeds in a bowl with 8 fluid ounces water and place the kumquat slices in a larger bowl with 50 fluid ounces water. Cover both and soak overnight in the refrigerator.

Preheat the oven to 275°F. Sterilize your glass jars and lids (see page 47).

Strain the soaking liquid from the seeds into a large pan and add the kumquats and their soaking liquid. Bring to a boil, then reduce to a simmer. Cover and simmer for 10 to 15 minutes until the kumquats are very tender. Remove the lid and keep simmering until the volume is reduced by half.

Meanwhile, warm the sugar in the oven on a baking sheet for 15 minutes. Tip the warm sugar and chopped rosemary into the pan and stir until the sugar is fully dissolved. Bring the mixture back to a rapid boil for 15 minutes.

Remove from the heat and transfer the marmalade to a pitcher. Carefully pour it into the warm, sterilized jars, filling them to about ¼ inch from the top. Tightly seal the jars and let cool completely. They will keep in a cool, dark place for up to 12 months. Once opened, store in the refrigerator for up to 3 months.

## TIPS

Make sure you start the marmalade-making process a day before you'd like to pop a jar open—it needs to soak overnight.

Like other seasonal citrus fruits, kumquats are only readily available in the winter months. Once you see them appear in stores, we recommend you stock up and make a few batches of this marmalade to see you through the year.

# Crumpets with Rhubarb and Orange Curd

Once you know how, crumpets are so satisfyingly easy to make! Like most homemade treats, they're also a whole lot tastier than the store-bought version. We love to generously spread our silky Rhubarb and Orange Curd (page 46) over each crumpet, bringing a fruity burst of flavor to every bite. You will need 4 to 6 metal crumpet or dessert rings, 2¾ inches in diameter, although a round metal cookie cutter will work too.

## MAKES 15 CRUMPETS

¾ fluid ounce whole milk
1 teaspoon superfine sugar
1 x ¼-ounce packet of active
   dry yeast
7 ounces white bread flour
3½ ounces all-purpose flour
½ teaspoon baking soda
½ teaspoon fine salt
1 ounce butter, melted,
   for greasing

Mix 7 fluid ounces warm water, the milk, and the sugar together in a pitcher (make sure the mixture is warm) and stir in the yeast. Leave for 10 to 15 minutes until the yeast has become frothy.

In a large mixing bowl, sift together the flours, baking soda, and salt and make a well in the middle. Tip in the warm milk and beat into the flour with a wooden spoon to form a smooth batter.

Cover the bowl with a dish towel or plastic wrap and leave the batter somewhere warm for 1 hour. It should have small bubbles all over the top when ready.

Thoroughly brush the inside edge of your metal rings and a large skillet with the melted butter, then heat the skillet over medium-low heat until the butter starts to bubble and sizzle. Fit as many metal rings as you can into the pan, sitting them flat on the bottom.

Spoon or pour the batter into the metal rings until each is half filled, then gently cook for 8 to 10 minutes until the tops are dry to the touch and covered in little holes.

Carefully push the crumpets from their metal rings onto a plate (you may need a knife to loosen them and a dish towel or oven mitt to protect your fingers from the heat), then place them back in the pan, upside down, to brown the tops for about 2 minutes.

Reheat and regrease the pan and rings and repeat the process of filling, cooking, and flipping until all the batter has been used up.

Either serve the crumpets warm, or let cool on a wire rack and toast before serving, with plenty of butter or our curd (see the recipe on page 46).

# Rhubarb and Orange Curd

Curds need to be cooked slowly over low heat, with constant stirring to prevent the eggs curdling or catching around the edge of the pan. Avoid the temptation to turn up the heat in a moment of impatience. Instead, slowly persist until you have a silky curd that coats the back of a spoon without running off.

**MAKES 2 X 9-OUNCE JARS**

14 ounces rhubarb, trimmed and chopped into ½-inch pieces

Finely grated zest of 1 orange

2½ fluid ounces freshly squeezed orange juice (from about 1 orange)

5¼ ounces superfine sugar

2 teaspoons cornstarch

2 extra-large eggs

1¾ ounces unsalted butter, cubed

A couple of drops of pink food coloring (optional)

Preheat the oven to 275°F. Sterilize jam jars: wash the jars and lids in soapy water, rinse well, then set them upside down on a baking sheet and place in the oven for 15 minutes.

Put the chopped rhubarb, orange zest, and juice into a small pan along with 1 tablespoon water and place over medium heat. Gently simmer for 10 minutes until the rhubarb is soft and has broken down.

Strain the rhubarb and all the juices through a strainer into a medium pan, pressing out any liquid from the rhubarb to leave just the fibers behind in the strainer (discard these).

In a small bowl, whisk together the sugar and cornstarch, then crack the eggs into the bowl and whisk them in. Add the mixture to the pan of juices and whisk until smooth. Add the cubed butter and food coloring (if using).

Place the pan over low heat and gently stir the curd with a wooden spoon for 7 to 10 minutes, making sure to catch any bits that are cooking from around the edges and bring them into the middle. Keep stirring over low heat until the mixture is thick enough to coat the back of the spoon—a little thicker than the consistency of custard.

Pour the curd into the sterilized jars and seal with the lids. Let cool completely before cracking open to spread on crumpets! It will keep in the refrigerator for up to 3 weeks.

# KENZEY'S STORY

Kenzey struggled to find positive opportunities to pursue a life of independence. Her time in the criminal justice system at a young age meant that by the time of her release she was at a social and economic disadvantage.

But this did not dampen her spirits for a better life. Kenzey always loved baking, so when she saw an article in a magazine about the training offered by Luminary Bakery, she immediately jumped at the chance.

*"Because of everything I had been through in my past, I knew that this was a great opportunity to give me more skills to bake, as well as help empower me and give me confidence."*

As Kenzey's confidence grew, so did her excitement in experimenting with different flavors. She no longer felt like her background or inexperience was holding her back as she pulled together basic ingredients like flour, sugar, and butter and transformed them into delicious baked goods—baking we saw as outstanding. So much so, that when we held a competition on the course to find a new baked good, Kenzey's Chocolate and Hazelnut Pretzels (see page 50) had our taste buds celebrating. We happily chose her as our winner. We loved the inspiration behind her recipe: childhood memories of visiting shopping malls and enjoying a warm pretzel as a treat with her family and friends.

# KENZEY'S
# Chocolate and Hazelnut Pretzels

As far as breads go, these pretzels are the simple indulgences that dreams are made of—and the perfect on-the-go treat for adults and children alike.

MAKES 8

**For the pretzels**
16 ounces white bread flour
1¼ ounces light brown sugar
½ teaspoon fine salt
1 x ¼-ounce packet of
    active dry yeast

1¾ ounces unsalted butter,
    melted
1 tablespoon vegetable or
    sunflower oil, for greasing
3 tablespoons baking soda
1 large egg, beaten with
    a pinch of salt
1¾ ounces chopped
    hazelnuts

Kosher or sea salt,
    for sprinkling

**For the dipping sauce**
2 fluid ounces whole milk
4¼ ounces chocolate
    hazelnut spread
½ teaspoon vanilla extract
½ teaspoon honey

To make the dough, weigh the flour and sugar into a large mixing bowl. Add the salt to one side of the bowl and the yeast to the other, making sure they don't touch (if the yeast comes into direct contact with the salt it can retard it and stop the dough from rising). Toss the salt in some of the flour surrounding it, do the same with the yeast, finally mixing them all together until combined.

Make a well in the middle of the flour and pour in 9¼ fluid ounces warm water and the melted butter. Mix with a bench scraper or wooden spoon until it comes together into a messy dough. Tip the dough and any remaining flour onto a clean counter and knead for 10 minutes until smooth and supple. You'll be able to tell when you have kneaded it enough with the "windowpane test" (see page 31).

Transfer the dough back into the bowl, cover with a damp dish towel or plastic wrap, and let rise in a warm place for about 1 hour until it has doubled in size.

Line a couple of large baking sheets with baking parchment and grease with the vegetable oil.

Once the dough has risen, knock out any large air bubbles from the dough and divide into 8 equal pieces (weighing about 3½ ounces each). Roll each piece of dough into a long sausage, about 12 inches long. Make each sausage into a large U shape, cross the ends over one another, then twist them around once before attaching them near to the base of the U, making the classic pretzel shape (see illustration).

Once shaped, move the pretzels to the prepared baking sheets and leave for 30 to 40 minutes until doubled in size again.

Meanwhile, preheat the oven to 400°F.

Pour a quart of water into a large pan and bring to a boil. Tip the baking soda into the pan and let it bubble up and settle back down. One at a time, gently lower the pretzels into the boiling water and boil for 20 seconds—they should float. Remove the pretzels from the water with a flat spatula and carefully lay them back onto the lined baking sheets.

Brush the top of each pretzel with the beaten egg and sprinkle with chopped hazelnuts and kosher or sea salt. Bake for 20 to 25 minutes until a deep golden brown.

To make the dipping sauce, warm the milk in a pan over medium heat, then whisk in the chocolate hazelnut spread, vanilla, and honey until smooth. Either drizzle the sauce over the baked pretzels or serve it in small dishes alongside the warm pretzels for dunking.

## TIP

Brushing breads or pastries with beaten egg before baking gives them a golden brown sheen, but sometimes the egg can be jellylike and hard to brush on without damaging the dough. To avoid this, beat a pinch of salt into the egg and set it aside for 5 to 10 minutes before brushing it on.

# OUR SIGNATURE
# Cinnamon Swirls with Cream Cheese Frosting

Our infamously large, gorgeously swirled cinnamon buns are one of our most popular bakes. Nothing compares to a fresh cinnamon bun—fluffy dough spiraled with sweet cinnamon butter and baked until puffy and golden. A few years ago, when we began baking these scrumptious swirls in our very first kitchen, we'd pile them high into large boxes and carry them on the Tube across London to cafés and their hungry customers. You can imagine the looks from commuters as the smell of freshly baked cinnamon pastries filled the carriages! Now our buns only have to make the short journey from the ovens to our counters at the Luminary Bakeries where they're sold fresh every day, warm and generously piped with luxurious cream cheese frosting.

**MAKES 8 LARGE BUNS**

**For the dough**
24 ounces white bread flour,
    plus extra for dusting
2½ ounces superfine sugar
1½ teaspoons salt
3¼ teaspoons active
    dry yeast
1 large egg, beaten
13½ fluid ounces whole milk,
    warmed to lukewarm

2½ ounces unsalted butter,
    softened

**For the filling**
5¼ ounces unsalted butter,
    softened
2¾ ounces light brown sugar
2¾ ounces light corn syrup
1 tablespoon ground
    cinnamon

**For the frosting**
1¾ ounces unsalted butter,
    softened
3½ ounces cream cheese,
    at room temperature
7 ounces confectioners' sugar
½ teaspoon vanilla extract

To make the dough, combine the flour and sugar in a large mixing bowl. Add the salt to one side of the bowl and the yeast to the other, making sure they don't touch. Toss the salt in some of the flour surrounding it and do the same with the yeast, finally mixing them all together until combined. (If the yeast comes into direct contact with the salt it can retard it and stop the buns rising.)

Weigh out 1 ounce of the beaten egg (about half—set the other half aside for an egg wash later) and mix into the warm milk. Make a well in the middle of the flour, pour in the milk mixture, and use a butter knife or bowl scraper to bring it together into a soft ball of dough. Get your hands involved, kneading it in the bowl before tipping it out onto a clean counter.

Knead the dough for 10 minutes, using a bench scraper to keep the counter clean. Avoid dusting it with extra flour (this will give you hard, tough buns). It will be very sticky so try slapping it on the counter and folding it over repeatedly, to keep it from covering every inch of the surface. Alternatively, use an electric mixer fitted with a dough hook to do all the messy kneading for you.

Add the butter to the dough and knead for another 5 minutes until glossy and still slightly sticky to the touch. Try the "windowpane test" (see page 31) to be sure it's ready. Return the dough to the mixing bowl, cover with a damp dish towel or plastic wrap, and leave somewhere warm to rise until doubled in size (1½ to 2 hours).

Meanwhile, make the filling. In a bowl, mix the butter, sugar, syrup, and cinnamon into a smooth paste using a wooden spoon or spatula. Spread about 2 tablespoons of the mixture over the base of a 12 x 10 x 2-inch baking pan and set aside.

Once the dough has risen, knock out the excess air by squashing and punching it back into the bowl a few times. Scrape the dough out onto a very well-floured counter and use a floured rolling pin to roll the dough out into a 23 x 12-inch rectangle, about ¾-inch thick.

Evenly spread the remaining filling mixture across the dough, right to the very edges. Take the short edge of dough and fold over ½ inch of it, then continue to gently roll the dough up into a tight swirl, using your fingers and thumbs to work from one side to the other. Roll it as tightly as possible. You should be left with a dough sausage about 12 inches in length.

Mark out, then use a very sharp knife to cut the sausage of dough into 8 even slices. Place the slices, swirl side facing up, on the cinnamon-smeared baking pan, spacing them about ¾ to 1¼ inches apart. Leave somewhere warm for 4 to 60 minutes to rise a second time, covered with a damp dish towel or plastic wrap. They should have doubled in size and started to touch one another.

Meanwhile, preheat the oven to 400°F.

Brush the top of each swirl with the remaining beaten egg, then bake for 20 to 25 minutes until golden brown. Once baked, transfer the pan to a wire rack and let them cool completely in the pan.

To make the frosting, beat together the softened butter and cream cheese with an electric mixer or spatula until smooth. Add the confectioners' sugar in 3 stages, mixing in each third before adding the next. Once it's smooth and creamy, mix in the vanilla extract. Spoon the frosting into a pastry bag and pipe zigzags over the top of each cooled bun. If you don't have a pastry bag, don't worry—you can use a spoon to drizzle or smear the frosting over the tops of the buns instead. Enjoy!

*"Hospitality is 'love on the loose.'*
*It means more than an occasion to*
*cook and consume, but to create*
*a welcoming space to empower*
*friendship, purpose, and unity.*
*With that, you are encompassing*
*the very best of the things that*
*Luminary represents."*

LIZ, LUMINARY TRUSTEE
AND DIRECTOR

# QUICK
# BREADS

As the name suggests, quick breads are surprisingly *quick* to make. Unlike yeasted breads, they don't require kneading or rising, so their doughs or batters can be made and put straight in the oven to bake. They rely on baking powder or baking soda instead of yeast to make them rise, so in place of yeast's familiar taste we pack in plenty of punchy flavors—think gooey cheese, roasted garlic, zesty orange, and warming cider.

These quick breads are a blessing on days where you don't have the time to wait around for homemade bread to be ready. And with mixing and shaping being the only skills required to make a loaf (and sometimes not even that!), they're much easier to master, too. You'll be whipping up a loaf in next to no time!

Better still, lots of quick breads don't need gluten (the stretchy protein found in flour) to give them their structure, so they can be easily adapted to use gluten-free (GF) flour. GF breads can be harder to come by, so celiacs or those on GF diets will find a few recipes in this chapter to enjoy.

# TRACEY'S STORY

Some people you meet in life just *sparkle*. From the first day we met Tracey, she captivated us with her stories. She grew with us just as we grew as an organization with her—in animation, experience, and boldness. A graduate of our first cohort, she has influenced Luminary's journey. Hers is, simply put, a story of rising hope!

Tracey spent a large part of her life in a home darkened by domestic violence. She was kept secluded away from the bright world outside and driven into a life of forced isolation. There were rare moments of genuine human connection and what she thought, liked, or disliked was not heard or even acknowledged. When she finally escaped, homelessness was the only option and she sought refuge in a hostel. While there, she was invited to a baking course at Luminary.

*"Luminary, for me, was a godsend. They gave me confidence and courage and a voice to speak. I hadn't spoken for two years, but then I came to Luminary. They gave me hope where there was no hope."*

Tracey eventually found her voice during the course at Luminary. Being around women who had similar backgrounds and living conditions drew out confidence and gave her a community of women to learn from and be encouraged by. During our personal and professional group sessions where the women learn how to grow in confidence and perception of their self-worth, Tracey began to find her voice. It wasn't easy at the time, and some days it felt daunting, but the support and space Tracey received helped her to process the past and seek a new hope for the future. Tracey began to trust again.

Although Tracey classified her first attempts at baking as "disastrous," she remained determined. As an avid cook, she quickly realized that baking relied on using specific measurements. Accuracy was key. Hers wasn't just a dedication to learn, but a courageous fight for a new and better life.

*"Luminary is love, trust, hope, and life!*
*You come in broken and you go out like a firework!"*

# LUMINARY'S
# Carrot Bread with Nigella Seeds

Inspired by Tracey's radiant story of perseverance, our carrot bread really does glow! Packed with orange carrots and yellow turmeric, it's a sunny recipe that will brighten the day of anyone who eats a slice ... or two!

**MAKES 1 LOAF**

3½ tablespoons unsalted butter,
    plus extra for greasing
1 small onion (4 ounces), finely
    chopped
½ teaspoon ground coriander
½ teaspoon ground cumin
¼ teaspoon ground turmeric
1 teaspoon nigella seeds,
    plus extra for sprinkling
5¼ ounces gluten-free white flour
3½ ounces fine cornmeal
1½ teaspoons gluten-free baking
    powder
½ teaspoon fine salt
½ teaspoon cracked black pepper
3 large eggs
5 fluid ounces whole milk
2 carrots (about 7 ounces), grated

Preheat the oven to 350°F. Grease and line a 2-pound loaf pan (8½ x 4½ x 2½ inches) with 2 strips of baking parchment, arranged in a cross shape overlapping on the bottom of the pan, to line every side.

Melt the butter in a small pan over medium heat, then add the chopped onion and gently fry for 5 to 10 minutes. Add the ground coriander, cumin, turmeric, and nigella seeds and cook, stirring, for 1 minute. Once they're soft and golden brown, set the onions aside to cool.

Sift the flour, cornmeal, baking powder, salt, and pepper into a large bowl and stir to mix.

In a separate medium bowl, whisk together the eggs and milk, then stir in the cooled onion and grated carrots.

Make a well in the middle of the dry ingredients and pour in the carrot mixture. Using a large spoon or spatula, bring the flour into the middle of the bowl, mixing it all together to form a batter. Once all the flour is incorporated, stop mixing and pour the batter into the lined loaf pan. Sprinkle a small handful of nigella seeds over the top.

Bake in the oven for 40 to 45 minutes until golden brown and an inserted skewer or knife comes out clean.

Let the bread cool in the pan for 5 minutes before tipping out onto a wire rack to cool completely. This is delicious eaten warm, spread with butter or dunked in soup.

### TIP
This bread is designed to work with gluten-free flour for those on gluten-free diets, but works just as well with all-purpose wheat flour.

# Cauliflower Cheese Savory Muffins

Our cheesy muffins contain comforting, warm spices and mustard. We should warn you though, once you've had one it's hard to resist going back for a second ...

MAKES 12

2¾ ounces unsalted butter
1 onion (4 ounces), finely
   chopped
1 teaspoon mustard powder
1 teaspoon curry powder
1 teaspoon black mustard
   seeds

9¾ ounces plain yogurt
3⅓ fluid ounces whole milk
2 large eggs
8¾ ounces all-purpose or
   gluten-free flour
2 teaspoons baking powder
½ teaspoon baking soda
1½ teaspoons fine salt

3½ ounces sharp cheddar
   cheese, grated, plus a
   little extra to sprinkle
   on top
9 ounces cauliflower,
   coarsely cut into
   ½- to ¾-inch pieces
Cracked black pepper

Preheat the oven to 400°F and line a 12-cup muffin pan with paper liners.

Melt the butter in a small skillet over medium heat, add the onion, and gently fry for 5 to 10 minutes until soft and golden brown. Sprinkle the mustard powder, curry powder, and black mustard seeds over the onion and fry for another 2 minutes, stirring regularly. Set aside to cool.

In a medium bowl, whisk together the yogurt, milk, and eggs, then stir in the cooled onion.

In a large bowl, sift together the flour, baking powder, baking soda, and salt, then stir in the grated cheese and chopped cauliflower. Make a well in the middle of the mixture and pour in the wet ingredients. Using a large spoon or spatula, bring the flour into the middle of the bowl, mixing it all together to form a stiff batter. Once all the flour is incorporated, stop mixing—overmixing will result in rubbery muffins!

Use a spoon or ice-cream scoop to evenly divide the muffin batter among the paper liners, filling them three-quarters full. Sprinkle over a little extra cheese and crack some black pepper over the top of each one.

Bake for 18 to 20 minutes until the muffins are golden brown and they spring back when gently pressed.

# Roasted Garlic Irish Soda Bread

We have to thank our former head baker Aine, with her resourcefulness and Irish roots, for introducing us to the wonders of Irish soda bread. We sell loaves of it at our café in Stoke Newington in London every day (usually still warm from the oven) and our customers often tell us that they can smell it cooking from down the street! It is one of the most versatile breads out there—you can add almost any ingredients you like. It is best eaten on the day that it's made, but makes great toast for days afterward, especially when slathered in salted butter.

MAKES 1 LOAF

1 bulb of garlic
1 tablespoon olive oil
14¼ fluid ounces buttermilk
    (or 10½ ounces yogurt
    and 4 fluid ounces whole
    milk mixed together)

8¾ ounces whole wheat flour
8¾ ounces all-purpose flour,
    plus extra for dusting
1 teaspoon baking soda
1 teaspoon fine salt
1 teaspoon cracked black
    pepper

Preheat the oven to 400°F and line a baking sheet with baking parchment.

Cut the top off the garlic bulb to just about reveal the cloves inside, leaving the papery skin on. Place the bulb in a small baking pan, drizzle with the olive oil, and bake in the oven for 20 to 30 minutes until the cloves are soft to the touch. Set aside to cool.

When cool, squeeze the roasted garlic out of each papery casing and into a separate bowl. Mash it up into a paste with a fork or press it through a garlic press, then mix in the buttermilk and whisk together.

In a large bowl, mix together the flours, baking soda, salt, and pepper, making sure the salt and baking soda are well distributed throughout the flour.

Make a well in the middle of the flour mixture and pour in the buttermilk mixture. Use your hands, a spatula, or bowl scraper to mix the wet ingredients into the dry until a sticky dough forms.

Lightly flour a counter and tip the dough onto it. Gently roll and fold the dough a couple of times to bring the mixture together. Do not knead—you just want to bring it together.

Shape the dough into a ball and transfer it to the baking sheet. Gently press down with your hands to flatten the ball into a disk, about 2 inches thick. Liberally dust the top with flour and use a large sharp knife to score the dough with a deep cross dividing it into quarters, about ¾ inch deep. A "sawing" action can help get a sharp cut.

Bake for 35 to 40 minutes until golden brown and hollow-sounding when turned upside down and knocked on the bottom. Once baked, let cool on a wire rack.

### TIP

This roasted garlic version is a favorite of ours, but if garlic isn't your thing, try adding 7 ounces of crumbled blue cheese and 3½ ounces of roasted walnuts instead—it's just as delicious and the oozy cheese is such a treat!

# Oat Milk Soda Bread

We love everything about soda bread: it's quick, easy, and cheap to make; it's a great use for milk that's turned sour; and there's no kneading or proofing required due to the absence of yeast. Usually, because of the lack of yeast that brings flavor to bread, it relies on tangy buttermilk as an ingredient—but we've developed this recipe using oat milk instead, so those on dairy-free diets can enjoy it too!

MAKES 1 LOAF

12 fluid ounces oat milk

2 tablespoons plus
   2 teaspoons lemon juice

7¾ ounces all-purpose flour,
   plus extra for dusting

7¾ ounces whole wheat flour

2¾ ounces rolled oats, plus
   some for topping

1½ teaspoons baking soda

1 teaspoon salt

Preheat the oven to 400°F and line a large baking sheet with baking parchment.

In a small bowl, combine the oat milk with the lemon juice and stir. Set aside for about 10 minutes to let it curdle slightly.

Weigh the flours into a large bowl, then add the oats, baking soda, and salt. Using your hands, rub the dry ingredients together, making sure the salt and baking soda are evenly distributed throughout the flour.

Make a well in the middle of the dry ingredients and pour in the curdled oat milk. Begin to fold the dry and wet ingredients together using a spatula or bowl scraper. The dough will feel very messy and possibly quite sticky, but avoid the temptation to add more flour. Keep on mixing until it resembles a rough, messy dough.

Flour your hands, turn the dough out onto a clean, well-floured counter, and bring the dough together into a ball. Transfer the ball

of dough to the lined baking sheet and flatten it with the palm of your hand to about 2 inches thick, sprinkling the top with more flour if it's sticking to your hands. Sprinkle a handful of oats over the top of the loaf.

Use a sharp knife to cut a deep cross into the loaf, about two-thirds of the way through, but not all the way to the sheet. A "sawing" action can help get a sharp cut. Let rest for 5 minutes.

Bake in the oven for 30 minutes until golden brown, well risen, and the loaf sounds hollow when turned upside down and tapped. Cool on a wire rack.

# Pumpkin and Chili Cornbread Muffins

Abby is one of the founding Luminary bakers and worked tirelessly to establish and run our first kitchen. She's particularly talented at making mouthwatering recipes for those with food intolerances and allergies. These golden muffins, influenced by her American upbringing, are testament to that—free from gluten, eggs, dairy, soy, nuts, and refined sugar—and yet absolutely packed full of flavor. There's no better companion to a big pot of chili.

MAKES 12

2 fluid ounces vegetable oil, plus extra for greasing
8½ fluid ounces plant-based milk (cashew, almond, soy, oat ... we use coconut)
2 teaspoons apple cider vinegar

2 red chiles (we use Thai chiles)
6 ounces fine cornmeal, plus extra for sprinkling
5¼ ounces gluten-free all-purpose flour
½ teaspoon baking soda
1½ teaspoons gluten-free baking powder

¾ teaspoon fine salt
1¾ tablespoons coconut sugar
3 ounces pumpkin puree (see tip)
2 ounces maple syrup, plus extra to serve (optional)

Preheat the oven to 325°F and brush the cups of a 12-cup muffin pan with a little oil.

In a small bowl, mix together the plant milk and apple cider vinegar and set aside for 5 to 10 minutes.

Meanwhile, carefully cut one of the chiles into thin rings, discard the seeds, and set the rings aside to decorate the top of the muffins. Seed and finely chop the second chile.

In a large bowl, mix together the cornmeal, flour, baking soda, baking powder, salt, and sugar.

In a separate bowl, mix together the pumpkin puree, vegetable oil and maple syrup with the milk and vinegar mixture.

Make a well in the middle of the dry ingredients and pour in the wet ingredients, mixing them until only a few lumps remain. Gently stir in the finely chopped chile and spoon the batter into the greased muffin pan, filling each cup about three-quarters full. Sprinkle the top of each with a little extra cornmeal and place a chile ring on top.

Bake in the oven for 18 to 20 minutes until the muffins spring back to the touch and an inserted toothpick comes out clean.

Let cool in the pan for 5 minutes before tipping them out onto a wire rack. Let them cool completely or serve them while they're still a bit warm, drizzled with a little maple syrup.

### TIP

You can use canned pumpkin or make your own pumpkin puree. To make your own: peel and cut a small pumpkin into 1-inch chunks. Steam it for 15 to 20 minutes until a fork slides through it easily without resistance. Add the pumpkin to a blender and gradually take the speed from low to high until it is pureed. Alternatively, use a potato masher to mash the pumpkin into a smooth puree.

# OUR SIGNATURE
# Cheese Scones with Savory Butter

Our head baker Rachel had one thing on her mind when planning the bakes for our first café: cheese scones. Really big, really fluffy, seriously cheesy scones. And they quickly became a firm favorite at Luminary. By nature, they're wonderfully quick and simple to make—easy crowd-pleasers that are both endearing and impressive to be pulling out of the oven if you have guests. Serve them warm and slathered with a butter flavored with yeast extract for a salty, savory treat.

MAKES 12

For the scones
31¾ ounces all-purpose flour, plus extra for dusting
2 tablespoons baking powder
1 teaspoon fine salt
1 teaspoon mustard powder
A generous pinch of cayenne pepper

3½ ounces unsalted butter, chilled, cut into ½-inch cubes
9 ounces sharp cheddar cheese, grated
9½ fluid ounces whole milk
1 large egg, beaten, or 1 tablespoon milk, for glazing
Cracked black pepper

For the savory butter
5¼ ounces salted butter, softened at room temperature
1½ ounces yeast extract, such as Marmite

Preheat the oven to 350°F and line a large baking sheet with baking parchment.

In a large bowl, mix together the flour, baking powder, salt, mustard powder, and cayenne pepper. Add the cubed butter and use your fingertips to rub the butter into the flour until only a few small lumps remain and it looks a bit like bread crumbs. Stir in 7 ounces of the grated cheese.

Make a well in the middle of the dry mixture and pour in the milk and 9½ fluid ounces cold water. Use a blunt butter knife to stir the dry mixture into the liquids until it starts to form a soft dough.

Once it's nearly combined, get your hands involved. Bring the dough together into a ball and tip out onto a floured counter, getting every last bit of flour out of the bowl. It might be stickier than you'd expect, but avoid the temptation to add more flour.

Liberally dust a rolling pin with flour and roll out the dough to about 1½ inches **thick. Use a 3½-inch round cutter to cut out circles of dough and place them on the lined baking sheet, about 2 inches apart. Reroll the scraps until you have used up all the dough.**

Brush the top of each scone with beaten egg or milk and sprinkle with the remaining 2½ ounces of grated cheese and some freshly cracked black pepper.

Bake for 20 to 25 minutes until well-risen and golden brown.

While the scones are in the oven, prepare the butter. Mix together the softened butter and yeast extract until marbled and swirly with glossy yeast extract streaks.

Once the scones are baked, leave for 5 minutes to cool slightly before serving with the salty savory butter. They're best eaten on the day they are made, and are exceptionally good when warm.

# Cider and Apple Bread

There's something striking about this cider and apple bread that'll remind you of the science at work when you bake. Adding the acidic apple cider vinegar to the alkaline baking soda sparks a magical instant reaction, producing gas and causing the mixture to foam and swell, leaving you with a light and fluffy loaf. It's a versatile bake that can be eaten at any time of day and becomes sweet or savory depending on what you choose to serve it with; great for breakfast spread with honey, or lunch alongside warming soups or stews.

MAKES 1 LOAF

Vegetable oil, for greasing
18 ounces all-purpose white
   flour, plus extra for
   dusting
1 teaspoon baking soda
½ teaspoon ground
   cinnamon
1 teaspoon fine salt
1 teaspoon apple cider
   vinegar
13½ fluid ounces cider
6 ounces grated
   eating apple
   (about 1 large
   or 2 small)

Preheat the oven to 400°F and grease and line a 2-pound loaf pan (8½ x 5½ x 2⅓ inches) with 2 strips of baking parchment, arranged in a cross shape overlapping on the bottom to line the sides of the pan.

In a large bowl, mix together the flour, baking soda, cinnamon, and salt, making sure all the ingredients are evenly distributed throughout.

In a separate bowl, mix together the vinegar, cider, and grated apple.

Make a well in the middle of the flour mixture and pour in the apple mixture. Using your hands, a spatula, or bowl scraper, work quickly to mix the wet ingredients into the dry until a sticky and foaming dough forms.

Tip the foamy batter into the loaf pan without knocking too much of the air out of it and sprinkle the top of the mixture with a handful of flour.

Bake for 35 to 40 minutes until golden brown and hollow-sounding when turned upside down and knocked on the bottom. Let cool on a wire rack.

This bread is best eaten on the day it's made, but makes great toast for days afterward.

# AINE'S

# Cranberry, Orange, and White Chocolate Soda Bread

Our former head baker Aine had a lasting impact on the Luminary trainees she taught to bake, encouraging self-worth and the therapeutic properties of baking. It was in the busy run-up to Christmas that she originally taught this heavenly recipe—it's quick to make and a great loaf for beginners. Packed with tart dried cranberries, orange zest, and creamy white chocolate, it's so delicious that we now happily eat it all year round!

**MAKES 1 LOAF**

8¾ ounces all-purpose flour, plus extra for dusting
8¾ ounces whole wheat flour
1 teaspoon baking soda
1¼ teaspoons fine salt
Grated zest of 1 orange
3½ ounces dried cranberries
3½ ounces white chocolate, coarsely chopped into ½-inch chunks
14¼ fluid ounces buttermilk (or 10½ ounces yogurt and 4 fluid ounces whole milk mixed together)

Preheat the oven to 400°F and line a baking sheet with baking parchment.

In a large bowl, mix together the flours, baking soda, salt, orange zest, dried cranberries, and white chocolate chunks, making sure the salt and baking soda are well distributed throughout the flour.

Make a well in the middle of the mixture and pour in the buttermilk. Using your hands, a spatula, or bowl scraper, mix the wet ingredients into the dry until a sticky dough forms.

Lightly flour a counter and tip the dough out onto it. Gently roll and fold the dough a couple of times to bring the mixture together. Do not knead—you just want to bring it together.

Shape the dough into a ball and transfer to the baking sheet, then gently press down on it with your hands to flatten the ball to a disk, about 2 inches thick.

Lightly dust the top of the dough with flour and use a large sharp knife to score a deep cross, about ¾ inch deep, into the top, dividing the dough into quarters.

Bake for 30 to 35 minutes until golden brown and hollow-sounding when turned upside down and knocked on the bottom. Let cool on a wire rack.

This bread is best eaten on the day it's made, but makes great toast for days afterward, especially when slathered in some salted butter.

COOKIES

As one of the first sweet treats we try as children, cookies have a special tie to childhood. Of the many bakes you could choose to make, these are on the simpler side, meaning they can be a fun activity to do with kids or are something novice bakers can turn to first. As a result, they joyously form some of our first baking memories—

*what* a great welcome to this world of flour, butter, and sugar!

For this reason, we start the Luminary Baking Program by making cookies—soft, almost fudgy in the middle, and golden and crisp on the outside. They are fun, they are delicious (sometimes *too* delicious), and they'll satisfy that sweet tooth, whatever the time of the day.

# KILIAN'S STORY

When Kilian was a child, hot homecooked meals were rare and there was no one around to explain how to combine ingredients into tasty treats. So, Kilian self-taught the only way a child could, by putting store-bought, readymade meals in the microwave. This continued into adulthood, but the inner ambition to seek better ways to cook and eat was never far away.

Years later, Kilian joined the Luminary Bakery program in the hope of a better life. Working alongside our bakery team, the support was a comfort. No longer alone in the learning process, trial-and-error became fun. It was through this collaborative effort that Kilian began to feel a bond with the other trainees. As someone who avoided sharing about the past, Kilian found that Luminary's group sessions offered opportunities for her to process the disadvantage she had experienced, and also for everyone to walk together in turning their lives around. It created a bond that Kilian called "breathtaking."

Now, with a growing desire to discover the most tempting flavor combinations, Kilian doesn't shy away from experimenting, especially when it came to creating the cookie recipe on page 84. By the time the sixth batch of attempts came through, Kilian said the taste was "like a choir singing in harmony—several tones coming together for something new." Kilian took fresh mint buttercream —classier than peppermint—and paired it perfectly with coconut cookies. We were in awe!

*"Luminary is* prima *(German for 'great'). I feel respected. I don't feel judged. It's very constructive and positive to do baking. They really believe in me here! Like sand in an oyster, life can feel tough and gritty; there are so many pressures and it's easy to feel as though it's all so hard; so negative; we should just give up. But like an oyster transforms a piece of sand into a beautiful shiny pearl, with a bit of determination, help, and support, we can all shine and become something beautiful too ... Luminary has been my oyster."*

# KILIAN'S
# Coconut and Fresh Mint Sandwich Cookies

**Simply put, Kilian's cookies taste like the holidays: soothing, scrumptious, and full of memories!**

### MAKES 15 SANDWICH COOKIES

**For the cookies**
4½ ounces unsalted butter, softened
7 ounces confectioners' sugar
1 large egg
5¼ ounces all-purpose flour

½ teaspoon baking soda
½ teaspoon fine salt
3½ ounces dried shredded coconut, plus extra to decorate

**For the buttercream filling**
3¼ ounces unsalted butter, softened

7 ounces confectioners' sugar
1 tablespoon whole milk
Green food coloring
**2 tablespoons** finely chopped mint leaves

Beat the softened butter with an electric mixer on medium speed for a couple of minutes. Tip in the sugar and continue to beat until they are creamed together and the mixture has turned pale and fluffy. Add the egg to the mixture and beat in.

In a small, separate bowl, mix together the flour, baking soda, salt, and dried shredded coconut. Add this dry mixture to the butter mixture in thirds, mixing between each addition, until a soft cookie dough forms. Cover the bowl with plastic wrap and refrigerate for 20 to 30 minutes.

Meanwhile, preheat the oven to 350°F and line 2 large baking sheets with baking parchment.

Weigh the dough into ¾-ounce pieces and roll gently into balls between the palms of your hands. You should get 30 balls from the mixture.

Tip some more dried shredded coconut into a small bowl and roll each ball of dough around in the coconut until well coated.

Place the balls on the lined baking sheets, leaving a gap of at least 2 inches between each one to let them spread.

Bake for 10 to 12 minutes until golden around the edges.

Let cool for 10 minutes on the baking sheet, before transferring to a wire rack to cool down completely.

To make the buttercream filling, whisk the softened butter with an electric mixer on medium speed for a couple of minutes. Add the confectioners' sugar, a spoonful at a time, making sure it's all mixed in before adding the next spoonful. Continue to beat until the mixture becomes pale and fluffy. Add the milk and a tiny amount of green food coloring (less is more!) and mix to get a pale mint-green color. Finally, mix in the chopped mint leaves.

Fill a pastry bag with the buttercream (or just use a small butter knife if you don't have one). Pipe or smear a circle of buttercream on the underside of half of the cooled cookies, right up to the edge. Fill in the middle of the circle with a little more buttercream and sandwich each one with another cookie to finish.

# Pink Grapefruit and Poppy Seed Cookies

Buttery and crumbly, these are a teatime triumph. Grapefruit zest is the zingiest of all the citrus fruits—the flavor dances on your tongue and lingers a little while longer than orange and lemon. This recipe is inspired by cookies that we used to sell, designed by our very first apprentice, lovingly dug out of the Luminary archives to honor her and all she has achieved since.

MAKES 24

8¾ ounces unsalted butter, softened
3 ounces superfine sugar
1¾ ounces confectioners' sugar
Grated zest of 1 pink grapefruit (any grapefruit will work well if you can't find a pink one!)

1 large egg
1½ teaspoons vanilla extract
11¾ ounces all-purpose flour, plus extra for dusting
½ teaspoon fine salt

3 tablespoons poppy seeds
2 tablespoons granulated sugar

Using an electric mixer, cream together the butter, superfine and confectioners' sugars, and grapefruit zest until light and fluffy, then beat in the egg and vanilla until fully combined.

On a slow speed, gradually add in the flour, salt, and 1 tablespoon of the poppy seeds and gently mix it into a speckled dough. Stop mixing as soon as there's no more flour visible.

Turn the dough out onto a clean, lightly floured counter and gently roll it into a log shape, about 12 x 4 inches. Wrap tightly in plastic wrap, twisting it at the ends to pull it tight. Place in the freezer for 30 to 60 minutes to rest and chill.

Preheat the oven to 350°F and line 2 baking sheets with baking parchment.

Tip the granulated sugar and remaining poppy seeds into a baking sheet with a rim, unwrap the dough, and roll it gently in the mixture to coat the outside.

Use a sharp knife to cut the log into 24 equal slices, each about ½ inch thick, and place them on the lined sheets at least 2 inches apart to allow for spreading.

Bake for 12 to 15 minutes until golden brown.

Let the cookies cool for 5 minutes on the sheets before transferring to a wire rack to cool completely.

# Apricot and Pistachio Thumbprint Cookies

Steeped in Luminary history, these cookies were one of many that Sarah made when she, Abby, and Alice established our bakery. Having many mouths to feed growing up, Sarah was familiar with baking on a large scale and remained undaunted by the task of rolling hundreds of cookies. The first year at Luminary Bakery was chaotic to say the least, yet she consistently led with grace and patience, and remained as cheerful as the sunny pools of apricot sitting atop these cookies.

MAKES 12

6 ounces unsalted butter,
    softened
3¾ ounces superfine sugar
1 teaspoon vanilla extract
1 tablespoon whole milk
8 ounces all-purpose flour
A pinch of fine salt
1¾ ounces shelled, unsalted
    pistachios, finely chopped
3 ounces apricot jam

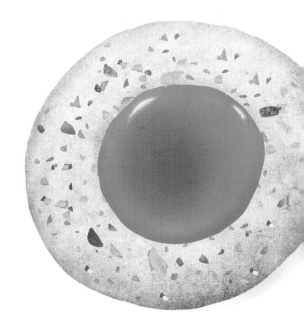

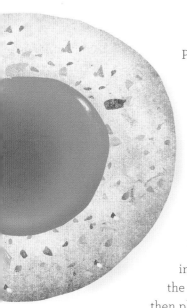

Preheat the oven to 350°F and line a large baking sheet with baking parchment.

Use an electric mixer to cream together the softened butter and sugar on medium speed. Once light and fluffy, add in the vanilla extract and milk and mix in, then add the flour and salt and mix on slow speed until it is a soft dough.

Tip the chopped pistachios into a small, separate bowl.

Use a tablespoon to scoop out chunks of dough from the bowl, weigh them at about 1½ ounces each, and roll gently into balls between the palms of your hands. Tip each ball into the chopped pistachios, rolling them around until well coated, then place on the lined baking sheet, spacing them 2 inches apart.

Bake for 10 minutes, then remove from the oven and make an indent in the middle of each cookie, pressing almost to the sheet underneath (see tip). The indent should be about ⅛ inch deep.

Place the cookies back in the oven for another 10 minutes until golden brown all over.

Let the cookies cool on the sheet. Once cooled, fill the indent in each cookie with a teaspoon of apricot jam.

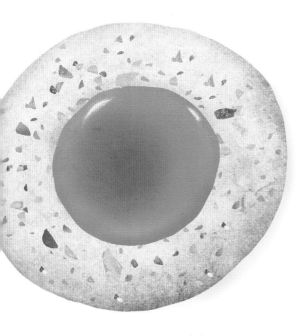

### TIP

Contrary to what the name suggests, we strongly recommend you *don't* use your thumb to make the indent in the middle of these cookies. Midway through baking, they'll be as hot as the sun! We tend to use the back of a tablespoon-size measuring spoon, but the end of a wooden spoon or a wine bottle cork will work well too.

# ALLISON'S
# Danish Snowball Cookies

Allison, a former team member at Luminary, has been making these cookies with her mom and grandma at Christmastime since she was small, but her family have been making them for generations. They would always agree to save some for Christmas morning, but if anyone couldn't resist pinching one, they would know from the telltale flurry of sugar "snow" they left behind!

MAKES 30

4 ounces unsalted butter, softened (substitute dairy-free margarine to make these vegan or dairy free)

6 ounces vegetable shortening, at room temperature
2 teaspoons vanilla extract
6 ounces confectioners' sugar
14 ounces all-purpose flour
1 teaspoon fine salt
4½ ounces walnuts, chopped

Using an electric mixer, mix together the butter, shortening, and vanilla extract until smooth and fully combined. Add 3½ ounces of the confectioners' sugar to the fats, a little at a time, and mix in.

Add the flour, salt, and chopped walnuts and mix together to combine. Cover the bowl with plastic wrap and refrigerate for 20 to 30 minutes.

Meanwhile, preheat the oven to 350°F and line a baking sheet with baking parchment. Use a tablespoon to scoop out chunks of dough from the bowl, weigh them at about 1 ounce each, and roll gently into balls between the palms of your hands. Place the balls on the lined baking sheet, spacing them 2 inches apart.

Bake for 20 to 25 minutes until the cookies are golden brown and firm to a gentle touch. Remove from the oven and let cool on the sheet for 3 minutes.

Tip the remaining 3 ounces of confectioners' sugar into a bowl.

While the cookies are still warm, roll each one in the bowl of confectioners' sugar until well coated, then let them cool completely on a flat surface.

When completely cool, roll each cookie in the confectioners' sugar for a second time and sift confectioners' sugar over the top so that they are fully coated before serving.

# Shortbread with an Espresso Twist

Some of the best recipes we know are family recipes—timeless classics, passed down from generation to generation, honed and refined by each new baker. Mim, a former baker at Luminary, was gifted a handwritten recipe book for her twenty-first birthday by her grandma, full to the brim with signature treats, such as this shortbread. Since then, Mim has fallen in love with Luminary's bespoke blend of espresso (courtesy of New Ground) and has used it to give her nanna's recipe an innovative new twist. It's a fantastic way to give a second life to leftover coffee grounds.

MAKES 10 TO 15
COOKIES

3½ ounces unsalted butter
2 teaspoons freshly ground
    espresso (or leftover
    coffee grounds, pressed
    of excess water)

3½ ounces all-purpose flour,
    plus extra for dusting
1¾ ounces rice flour
1¾ ounces superfine sugar,
    plus extra (optional) to
    decorate

3½ ounces dark chocolate
    (70% cocoa solids)
    (optional), to decorate

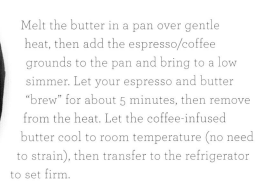

Melt the butter in a pan over gentle heat, then add the espresso/coffee grounds to the pan and bring to a low simmer. Let your espresso and butter "brew" for about 5 minutes, then remove from the heat. Let the coffee-infused butter cool to room temperature (no need to strain), then transfer to the refrigerator to set firm.

Cut the now-firm espresso butter into cubes.

Sift the flours into a large mixing bowl and add the superfine sugar and the espresso butter cubes. Rub the butter into the flour (alternatively, use an electric mixer on slow speed), mixing until the ingredients come together to form a ball of crumbly, speckled dough.

Wrap the dough in plastic wrap and chill in the refrigerator for 30 minutes.

Meanwhile, preheat the oven to 300°F and line a large baking sheet with baking parchment.

Remove the dough from the refrigerator and gently roll out on a floured counter to about ¼ inch thick. Use cookie cutters to cut out shapes and transfer these to the lined baking sheet.

Gently prick each shortbread cookie once with a fork.

Bake the shortbread for 35 to 40 minutes until pale golden brown.

You can either sprinkle the cookies with a little superfine sugar while they are still warm from the oven and let cool completely, or follow the directions below to decorate with chocolate.

Place two-thirds of the chocolate in a small microwaveable bowl and melt it in the microwave, heating for 30 seconds at a time, and stirring between each stage. When it has only just melted, tip in the remaining chocolate and stir until it's completely melted and shiny. This technique is a cheat's version of tempering called "seeding"— it should give you shinier chocolate than just melting it all together.

Half-dip each shortbread cookie into the chocolate, then let set on a sheet of wax paper.

# White Chocolate and Black Sesame Cookies

These are cookies of contrast—the earthy, bitter black sesame seeds are brought together with creamy, sweet white chocolate, creating a beautiful blend of taste and texture that we find irresistible.

**MAKES 15 COOKIES**

5¾ ounces unsalted butter

1½ ounces superfine sugar

4½ ounces light brown sugar

1 large egg

1 teaspoon vanilla extract

1½ ounces light corn syrup

8¾ ounces all-purpose flour

1 teaspoon baking soda

½ teaspoon fine salt

1 ounce cornstarch

3½ ounces white chocolate chips or a bar cut into ½-inch chunks (white chocolate buttons are good in this recipe)

1 tablespoon black sesame seeds

Melt the butter in the microwave (or in a small pan over low heat) until liquid but not hot and spitting.

Using an electric mixer or whisk, mix the melted butter, superfine sugar, and brown sugar on medium speed until they're well combined and the butter no longer separates. It should look rather like a thick caramel.

Add the egg, vanilla, and light corn syrup and beat until thoroughly mixed, scraping down the sides of the bowl with a spatula as needed.

In a small, separate bowl, weigh out the flour, baking soda, salt, and cornstarch, then sift this over the egg mixture.

On slower speed, mix the flour into the batter until it resembles a soft dough and there are no pockets of flour remaining. Tip in 3 ounces of the white chocolate chips and stir gently into the dough. Don't overmix once the chocolate chips are added or you'll get a tough cookie!

Tip the black sesame seeds into a small bowl or saucer and line a couple of large baking sheets with baking parchment.

Use a tablespoon to scoop out chunks of cookie dough from the bowl, weigh them at about 1¾ ounces each, and roll gently into balls between your hands. Lightly dip the top of each ball into the black sesame seeds and place, sesame side up, on the lined baking sheets, spacing them about 2 inches apart. Stick 2 to 3 of the remaining white chocolate chips on the top of each ball. Place the sheets of cookie balls in the refrigerator to chill for 20 to 30 minutes.

Meanwhile, preheat the oven to 350°F.

Bake for 8 to 10 minutes until the cookies have spread out and are golden around the edges but still slightly pale in the middle. Avoid the temptation to bake them until deep golden brown all over—they might look under-cooked in the middle, but will give you a gloriously chewy center once they have cooled.

Let the cookies cool on the sheets for 10 minutes before transferring to a wire rack to cool completely.

## TIP

These cookies also bake perfectly, if not better, from frozen. This allows you to make a large batch in advance and bake them as and when you need (or bake a single cookie on one of *those* days, when an oven-warm cookie is the only cure). We recommend rolling them into balls and freezing in an airtight container for up to 3 months. When required, preheat the oven, pop them on a lined baking sheet, and bake for 10 to 12 minutes.

# Malted Chocolate Cookies

These are as fuss-free and fun to make as they are tasty. Using simple pantry ingredients and requiring you to roll the dough into a long sausage, they're an entertaining baking activity to do with kids. If you can resist eating all the dough before it's baked, we're sure you'll love the malty milk-chocolate reward that comes out of the oven.

**MAKES 24 SMALL COOKIES**

4½ ounces unsalted butter, softened
2¼ ounces light brown sugar
4½ ounces all-purpose flour
1 teaspoon baking powder
1¾ ounces malted milk powder
¾ ounce unsweetened cocoa powder
A pinch of fine salt

Preheat the oven to 325°F and line a large baking sheet with baking parchment.

Cream together the softened butter and light brown sugar until pale and fluffy.

In a separate bowl, sift together the flour, baking powder, malted milk powder, cocoa, and salt.

Gently mix the flour mixture into the butter mixture until a soft dough forms, being careful not to fling flour everywhere in the process!

Once a soft dough has formed, tip it out onto a clean counter. Roll the dough into a long log, about ¾ inch thick and 39 inches long (or do it in sections, rolling a quarter of it at a time).

Using a sharp knife, cut the dough log into 24 even pieces, each about 1½ inches long (during baking, these mini logs melt down to make rounded rectangular cookies). Lift each piece onto the lined baking sheet, spacing them ¾ inch apart.

Bake for 15 to 20 minutes until firm to the touch.

Let cool on the sheet for 5 minutes before transferring to a wire rack to cool completely.

# MIM'S
# Vegan Chocolate and Sea Salt Cookies

When Mim joined us, she not only brought a wealth of cake-decorating experience and a kind and caring spirit, but a passion for making exquisite vegan treats. Mim says this recipe is inspired by all the women she has worked with in the kitchen over the years—resilient, strong, and incredible. You'll savor every bite of these lightly salted cookies!

## MAKES 15

4 fluid ounces olive oil

2 fluid ounces cold water

7½ ounces light brown sugar

½ teaspoon vanilla extract

8¾ ounces all-purpose flour

1 ounce unsweetened cocoa
    powder

1 teaspoon baking powder

¾ teaspoon baking soda

¼ teaspoon fine salt

6 ounces vegan dark
    chocolate (70% cocoa
    solids) chips or a bar cut
    into ½-inch chunks

Sea salt or kosher salt

Mix together the oil, water, sugar, and vanilla until the mixture is thoroughly combined and looks like caramel.

In a separate bowl, sift together the flour, cocoa, baking powder, baking soda, and salt.

Tip the dry ingredients into the wet ingredients and mix to fully combine and create a soft dough.

Add the chocolate chips and mix until equally distributed. Cover the bowl with plastic wrap and chill for 30 to 60 minutes until firm.

Preheat the oven to 350°F and line 2 large baking sheets with baking parchment.

Use a tablespoon to scoop out balls of dough onto the sheets, spacing them 2 inches apart to allow for spreading. Alternatively, weigh out balls of dough at 2 ounces each, and roll them in your hands before placing on the sheets. Top each cookie with a pinch of salt.

Bake for 10 to 12 minutes until the cookies have firmed up around the edges.

Let cool on the sheets for 5 minutes before transferring to a wire rack to cool completely.

# BARS AND SHEET CAKES

The sustenance of a homemade treat, the comfort of freshly baked brownies, the blissful indulgence of millionaire's shortbread ... these will always have a subtle familiarity and an ease for sharing. The aromas of the bakes you'll find in these pages have the ability to create an atmosphere of home. Ranging from sweet apples and warming spices to sharp lemon zest and buttery shortbread, they'll fill your home as you bake—an inviting welcome to anyone who steps through the door. These are everyday goodies —they don't require a celebration or special occasion, fancy equipment, or grand decoration. Instead, they're treats to be shared and savored in life's little moments and on everyday adventures.

# GRACE'S STORY

The atmosphere of a supportive and comforting home is one that Luminary aims to create as we welcome apprentices like Grace to the bakery. This is her story.

After coming out of a refuge and being placed in a hostel, the overwhelming task of creating a new life stood in front of Grace. On her own, lacking family and support, Grace's main focus was providing for her daughter, Arya, and tackling the impending questions around basic necessities for provision. But when she came across Luminary's story in a magazine, she was reminded of her harbored dreams of becoming a pastry chef and knew that we had the potential to offer the support she was seeking and needing.

Grace's kindhearted exuberance for a better life filled the rest of the women in her Luminary cohort with determination! Her enthusiasm for trying new ingredients and experimenting with flavors is why we called upon her as an apprentice to help create a new treat to be sold at Ben & Jerry's Scoop Shop in Soho, London. She began experimenting and until she made it perfect she wasn't going to give up—it took her nearly 20 tries to get it right. The result is on page 104.

Since graduating, Grace has returned to Luminary to work in the bakery. Her perseverance and boldness continues as she explores different ingredients and flavors, going above and beyond what is expected to create treats of genius.

*"No matter what happens at Luminary or with the apprentices, no matter what gets thrown at anyone, things will always be picked up and carried on. No one ever gives up! You'll always be able to look back—even if it's a month or a year—and see how much has changed. Nothing ever stays the same. There's always opportunity for growth—positive growth."*

# GRACE'S
# *Honeycomb Cheesecake Blondies*

**For Arya**

Grace explored many textures and tastes during the development of this recipe, but there was something that always drew her back to honeycomb—with its appeal of caramel, but lighter balance and crunchy twist. For Grace, this felt particularly nostalgic, reminding her of flavors she experienced as a child. It took her nearly 20 tries to get it right, but she persevered: "There's something in perseverance that reminds me of Arya, my daughter—she's everything I love!" The resulting melt-in-the-mouth blondies were well worth it.

MAKES 12 GENEROUS
SLICES

### For the honeycomb
Vegetable or sunflower oil,
    for greasing
1¾ ounces superfine sugar
1 ounce light corn syrup
½ teaspoon baking soda

### For the blondie batter
11¾ ounces unsalted butter,
    plus extra for greasing
3 large eggs
11¾ ounces brown sugar
1 teaspoon vanilla extract
11¾ ounces all-purpose flour
1½ teaspoons baking soda
½ teaspoon fine salt

### For the cheesecake swirl
6 ounces whole cream
    cheese
1 large egg yolk
¾ ounce confectioners'
    sugar
½ teaspoon vanilla extract

First, make the honeycomb. Line a deep baking sheet with baking parchment and smear with a little oil.

Tip the sugar and light corn syrup into a deep pan and place over low heat, swirling every now and again until all of the sugar has dissolved (you don't want it to bubble at this stage).

Once the sugar has melted, turn the heat up to medium, bring to a simmer, and keep swirling for 2 to 5 minutes until it turns a deep amber color. At this point, immediately take the pan off the heat and beat in the baking soda with a spatula. It will start to foam and rise in the pan. Continue to mix for a few more seconds, then scrape the mixture out onto the oiled sheet (be careful as the mixture will be very hot).

Set aside for at least 30 minutes—the honeycomb will continue to foam and grow and will eventually set rock hard.

Preheat the oven to 350°F. Line the bottom of an 9 x 9-inch baking pan with baking parchment, greasing the sides with butter.

To make the blondie batter, melt the butter in the microwave or in a small pan over low heat until liquid but not hot and spitting.

In a separate bowl, beat together the eggs, sugar, and vanilla extract. Once the butter has melted, add it to the egg mixture and gently whisk until smooth and glossy.

In another small bowl, mix together the flour, baking soda and salt. Tip this into the glossy mixture and mix until there are no pockets of flour remaining.

Break the honeycomb up into ¾- to 1¼-inch chunks and add to the blondie batter. Briefly stir through, then scrape it into the lined pan, spreading it flat.

In one final bowl, make the cheesecake swirl. Mix together the cream cheese, yolk, confectioners' sugar, and vanilla until smooth.

Dollop large blobs of the cheesecake mixture across the top of the blondie batter, then use a butter knife to swirl it into the batter to give a marbled effect on the top.

Bake for 40 to 45 minutes until golden brown all over but still a bit wobbly in the middle (the wobble is crucial, otherwise you'll have dry, cakey blondies). Once baked, let cool completely in the pans before cutting into 12 squares and tucking in!

# IDA'S
# Honey and Walnut Drizzle Cake

Prior to her arrival at Luminary, Ida* had been living in a safehouse after experiencing gender-based violence. English was not her first language and so she was shy at first, but very quickly her innovation with ingredients inspired us all. Coming from a disadvantaged background, Ida had to work hard at a very young age to put together the pieces she needed to complete a recipe—even churning her own butter. Although her family didn't have a lot of options, for Christmas and New Year they would always make *shendetlie*, one of the finest seasonal bakes in Albania and the inspiration behind Ida's traybake recipe. Every year, her family would look forward to this luxurious treat. With mouthwatering ingredients such as honey and walnuts enhancing the cake's flavor, it shouldn't be a surprise if you find people competing for the first taste!

MAKES 16 SLICES

**For the cake**
4½ ounces unsalted butter, melted, plus extra for greasing

2 large eggs plus 1 yolk
4½ ounces superfine sugar
7 ounces honey
10½ ounces plain yogurt
14 ounces all-purpose flour
2 teaspoons baking soda

6 ounces walnuts, finely chopped

**For the syrup**
9½ ounces superfine sugar
3½ ounces honey

*Name changed to protect identity

Preheat the oven to 350°F. Grease a deep 9 x 9-inch baking pan with a little butter and line the bottom with baking parchment.

Combine the eggs, egg yolk, and sugar in a large bowl and whisk together until pale, frothy, and slightly thickened.

Whisk in the butter and honey, followed by the yogurt.

Sift the flour and baking soda over the mixture and stir in until no lumps of flour remain.

Fold the chopped walnuts into the batter and pour it into the prepared pan. Let rest for 10 minutes.

Bake in the oven for 45 to 50 minutes until dark golden brown and the sponge springs back to the touch. Set aside to cool in the pan.

While it cools, make the syrup. Combine 9¼ fluid ounces water, the sugar, and honey in a pan and bring to a boil. Reduce to a gentle simmer and cook for 15 to 20 minutes until it has reduced to a runny, slightly syrupy consistency.

Leaving the cake in the pan, use a sharp knife to cut the cake into diamonds, slicing it in intersecting diagonal lines, 2 inches apart.

Pour the hot syrup over the cake and let it soak in for at least 30 minutes before serving, although it's even better if left to mature for a day.

# RACHEL'S
# Apple, Rosemary, and Brown Butter Blondies

These blondies are the first thing that Rachel, our former head baker and trainer, baked for Alice and the team when she joined Luminary. They always take us back to those early days. We love the salty-sweet contrast in the blondie batter—the soft juicy apples, surrounded by comforting cinnamon and fresh rosemary. They're one of Rachel's favorite and most-baked recipes and everything we adore in one squidgy square!

### MAKES 12

6¾ ounces unsalted butter, plus extra for greasing

2 extra-large eggs

3½ ounces dark brown sugar

3½ ounces light brown sugar

3¾ ounces superfine sugar

1½ teaspoons vanilla extract

6 ounces all-purpose flour

1 teaspoon baking powder

1 teaspoon fine salt

1½ teaspoons ground cinnamon

3½ ounces dark chocolate (70% cocoa solids), cut into chunks

2 eating apples (10 to 12 ounces total), chopped into ½-inch chunks

1 tablespoon finely chopped fresh rosemary (3 sprigs)

Preheat the oven to 350°F and grease and line an 9 x 9-inch baking pan with a little butter and baking parchment.

First, make your brown butter—also known as *beurre noisette*. Melt the butter in a small pan with a light-colored bottom (if possible) over gentle heat, then turn up the heat and let it bubble for 5 to 10 minutes. Watch it like a hawk—the milk solids can easily burn if left for too long. The butter will start to bubble and might spit a little—this is okay—then it will start to foam and you will be unable to see below the thick froth. Keep heating, swirling the pan from time to time, until it smells nutty and fragrant and the butter has turned an amber color. Take it off the heat and pour into a large bowl, making sure you scrape the brown bits into the bowl as well—these are the cooked milk solids that have caramelized on the bottom of the pan and they give the butter its delicious nutty, caramel flavor. Set aside to cool for about 5 minutes.

Add the eggs, sugars, and vanilla to the cooled butter and beat with an electric mixer for about 5 minutes until pale and thick.

Sift the flour, baking powder, salt, and cinnamon over the top of the mixture and gently fold it in until no lumps of flour remain.

Finally, mix in the chopped chocolate, apple, and rosemary. Pour the batter into the baking pan and smooth it out with a spatula.

Bake for 45 to 50 minutes until an inserted toothpick comes out clean. These blondies don't want a wobble in the middle, they should be reasonably firm when pressed.

Let the blondies cool completely in the pan before turning out and cutting into 12 pieces.

# GRACE'S
# Masala Chai and Berry Crumble Cake

The comforts of crumble cakes never cease to amaze. This was our exact reaction when Grace, one of our wonderful Luminary graduates, presented us with this cake while completing her apprenticeship in our bakery. Wow! Its bold chai influence came from two years of new discoveries with us after being disconnected from the world around her (after taking shelter in a refuge). One of those new discoveries was the chai latte, which inspired this far-too-tempting recipe. It's the perfect early fall cake, using the last of the summer fruits and comforting spices that hint toward the festive season ahead. It's a Sunday in your PJs, eating crumble, and thinking "everything is going to be fine" kind of cake.

MAKES 12 PIECES

**For the sponge**
5¼ ounces unsalted butter, softened, plus extra for greasing
8 cardamom pods
1 teaspoon fennel seeds
10 black peppercorns

2½ fluid ounces whole milk
5¼ ounces light brown sugar
3 large eggs
6 ounces self-rising flour
1 teaspoon ground cinnamon
½ teaspoon ground ginger
A pinch of ground cloves
1 teaspoon vanilla extract
5¼ ounces frozen berries

**For the crumble topping**
3½ ounces cold unsalted butter, cubed
5¼ ounces all-purpose flour
3½ ounces light brown sugar
A pinch of fine salt
3½ ounces frozen mixed berries

Preheat the oven to 350°F and grease and line an 9 x 9-inch baking pan with baking parchment.

Put the cardamom pods, fennel seeds, and peppercorns into a mortar and pestle and bash to a spicy rubble. Alternatively, tip them into a plastic freezer bag and bash them with a rolling pin.

Tip the spice rubble into a small pan along with the milk and bring to a gentle simmer. As soon as it starts simmering, remove the pan from the heat and set aside to cool and stew.

In a large bowl, cream together the softened butter and sugar until light and fluffy (use an electric mixer if you have one). Tip in the eggs, one at a time, thoroughly beating in before adding the next.

Sift the flour, cinnamon, ginger, and cloves over the mixture and fold in until no floury patches remain.

Strain the cooled spiced milk into the bowl through a fine strainer and stir into the batter along with the vanilla.

Finally, stir the frozen berries through the mixture and spoon it into the lined baking pan, spreading it out with a spatula.

Make the crumble topping by rubbing the cold butter into the flour with your fingertips until it resembles bread crumbs. Stir the sugar and salt through the crumble until well combined.

Sprinkle the crumble topping across the top of the cake batter, followed by the berries.

Bake for 35 to 40 minutes until the cake is golden brown and an inserted skewer comes out clean. The cake should spring back to the touch.

Let cool completely in the pan, before cutting into 12 equal pieces.

# MIMI'S

# Cardamom Millionaire's Shortbread

Mimi is a skilled freelance writer and a brilliant storyteller. She was a baker for Luminary between jobs and expert at giving her baking a creative twist, too. We love her take on a traditional millionaire's shortbread, with its crumbly cocoa base, cardamom vegan caramel, and a glossy layer of dark chocolate—it's deliciously distinctive!

MAKES 12 PIECES

**For the shortbread base**
4½ ounces dairy-free
    margarine, softened
1½ ounces superfine sugar
6½ ounces all-purpose flour
1 teaspoon unsweetened
    cocoa powder
A pinch of fine salt

**For the cardamom caramel**
3½ ounces dark brown sugar
¾ ounce dairy-free
    margarine
1 teaspoon ground
    cardamom (or seeds from
    8 large pods, ground in a
    mortar and pestle)
14 fluid ounces coconut
    cream

**For the chocolate topping**
7 ounces dark chocolate
    (70% cocoa solids),
    broken into pieces
1 ounce coconut oil

Preheat the oven to 350°F and line an 9 x 9-inch baking pan with baking parchment.

Start with the shortbread base. Beat the margarine and sugar together in a bowl until light and fluffy, then gradually sift in the flour, cocoa, and salt, beating it in until a soft, pastelike dough has formed. Tip the dough into the lined pan, pressing it down evenly over the bottom with your hands, and prick the surface all over with a fork.

Bake in the oven for 15 to 20 minutes until the shortbread looks dry on the top and is firm to the touch. Let cool.

Meanwhile, make the caramel. Combine the sugar and 1⅓ fluid ounces water in a pan over medium heat. Let the sugar dissolve and eventually turn to caramel. Don't stir! If you can't stand idly by and watch the caramel bubble into life, you can gently shake the pan a little.

After 5 to 6 minutes the caramel should be bubbling and caramelizing. Once all the water has evaporated and the mixture is forming thick bubbles, whisk in the margarine and cardamom.

Pour in the coconut cream, whisking continuously to form a smooth, runny caramel. Turn the heat down to low and continue cooking for 20 to 30 minutes, whisking from time to time, until the caramel becomes noticeably thicker and darker. It's ready when it thickly coats the back of a spoon and sets thick when you dollop a little bit onto a cold plate.

Take the pan off the heat and pour the caramel over the cooled shortbread base. Use a spatula to spread it smoothly across the entire base and right into the corners. Let cool completely.

To make the chocolate topping, melt the chocolate and coconut oil together in a heatproof bowl set over a pan of simmering water (don't let the bottom of the bowl touch the water). Alternatively, gently melt them in the microwave, being careful to stop and stir the mixture every 30 seconds to avoid burning it.

Pour the smooth shiny chocolate topping over the cooled caramel and chill in the refrigerator for 1 to 2 hours until set.

Use a sharp knife to gently cut the shortbread into 12 even slices. Try not to eat them all yourself—or at least not in one sitting!

### TIP

This recipe calls for coconut cream—the thicker, creamier friend of canned coconut milk. It's usually found in cartons in the Asian foods section of grocery stores. We wouldn't recommend using coconut milk instead, as it's a lot more watery and won't set the caramel.

# Ginger Tiffin with Candied Ginger

You can think of this tiffin as Rocky Road's older, more sophisticated sister. Laden with fiery candied ginger and crunchy ginger cookies, it's an indulgent treat to be taken seriously!

**MAKES 20 SQUARES**

10½ ounces dark chocolate
    (70% cocoa solids),
    broken into pieces
4½ ounces dairy-free
    margarine
1¾ ounces light corn syrup
½ teaspoon salt
12¼ ounces ginger cookies
2¼ ounces candied ginger,
    cut into ¼-inch pieces

Line an 9 x 9-inch baking pan with baking parchment.

Set a heatproof bowl over a pan of simmering water (don't let the bottom of the bowl touch the water). Add the chocolate, margarine, light corn syrup, and salt to the bowl and let them melt together, slowly stirring from time to time.

Meanwhile, place the ginger cookies in a plastic freezer bag and crush with a rolling pin until you have a mixture of larger pieces, crumbs, and dust. Alternatively, briefly blitz them in a food processor.

Once the chocolate mixture has completely melted and is smooth and glossy, remove it from the heat. Tip in the ginger cookie rubble and candied ginger and stir until well combined.

Tip the chocolatey mixture into the lined pan and use the back of a spoon to gently press it into the pan, making sure to get right into the corners. Cover and chill in the refrigerator for 1 to 2 hours until set.

Once firm, cut into 20 equal squares.

# RACHEL'S
# Praline and Cream Brownies

Whether part of a celebration or a treat to mark the end of a long and hard day, moments of indulgence can make life lighter and that little bit sweeter. Fudgy with rich chocolate, caramel, silky cream cheese, and toasted nuts, Rachel's brownies are as decadent as it gets!

MAKES 12

Unsalted butter, for greasing
2¾ ounces pecans

**For the cream cheese swirl**
8 ounces cream cheese,
    at room temperature
1 large egg yolk
2¾ ounces superfine sugar
A couple of drops of
    vanilla extract

**For the caramel swirl**
2¼ ounces superfine sugar
1½ ounces light corn syrup
1 tablespoon unsalted butter
1⅓ fluid ounces heavy cream

**For the brownie batter**
3 ounces unsalted butter
3½ ounces dark chocolate
    (70% cocoa solids),
    broken into pieces
4½ ounces superfine sugar

2 large eggs
1 teaspoon vanilla extract
2½ ounces all-purpose flour
    (gluten-free also works
    well here)
1½ tablespoons unsweetened
    cocoa powder
⅛ teaspoon fine salt

PRALINE AND CREAM BROWNIES

Preheat the oven to 350°F. Line the bottom of an 9 x 9-inch baking pan (or a slightly smaller one, if you'd like deeper brownies) with baking parchment and grease the sides with butter.

Tip the pecans onto a baking sheet and pop them into the oven for 10 minutes to toast. They'll start to smell fragrant when they're ready.

Meanwhile, make the cream cheese swirl. Beat together the cream cheese, egg yolk, sugar, and vanilla until smooth and set aside.

To make the caramel swirl mixture, melt the sugar and light corn syrup in a small, heavy-bottomed pan over low heat, swirling to dissolve all the sugar—do not stir! Turn the heat up to medium and continue to swirl the pan every now and again until you have a deep copper-colored caramel. Reduce the heat to low, then gradually whisk the butter into the pan in small pieces, followed by the cream—it will spit a little to start with, so be careful! Once smooth and glossy, set aside to cool and firm up a little.

To make the brownie batter, melt the butter and chocolate together in a heatproof bowl set over a pan of simmering water (don't let the bottom of the bowl touch the water). Alternatively, gently melt them in the microwave, being careful to stop and stir the mixture every 30 seconds to avoid burning it.

Beat the sugar into the chocolate mixture, followed by the eggs and vanilla.

In a small, separate bowl, mix together the flour, cocoa powder, and salt until completely combined and uniform in color. Sift this into the brownie batter and mix in until the mixture is glossy and there are no more pockets of flour.

Break up the toasted pecans in your hands so you have some whole ones and some rubble, and stir half of them through the brownie batter. Pour the brownie batter into the lined pan and spread flat with a spatula. Dollop both the cream cheese and caramel swirl mixtures in about 8 blobs on top of the batter and swirl it in using a butter knife. Sprinkle the remaining pecans across the top and tap the baking pan on the counter to flatten it all out.

Bake for 25 to 30 minutes until the middle has a little wobble but the edges feel firm (the wobble is crucial, otherwise you'll have dry brownies). Let cool completely in the pan. Cut into 12 squares.

# MATILDA'S STORY

The pursuit of happiness is never far from most people's minds. For Matilda, it was a never-ending struggle, without the right to work. For seven years, it seemed as though time stood still for Matilda, until she received the news that she had been accepted into Luminary's program. Then, hope began to rise.

Every single day, come rain or shine, Matilda made it to each training session. On one particular morning, she had fallen down the stairs and ended up in the ER. Even so, in typical Matilda style, she showed up to training in the afternoon on crutches!

After graduating from Luminary, Matilda went on to college, where she studied Level 3 Patisserie and Confectionery. We proudly celebrated with her as she graduated in 2020 with her certificate!

"It's not just baking—Luminary makes you feel at home, like family. We celebrate together! Everything everyone does means you're not alone. And I'm happy—baking makes me happy! I'm proud to say I am one of the Luminary girls!"

# MATILDA'S
# No-Bake "Caramel" Nut Bars

Matilda's hope and courage spurred her on to create this amazing no-bake recipe for Luminary. They're a bold treat, full of fruity, nutty goodness, and excellent as an afternoon pick-me-up!

**MAKES 10 BARS**

**For the base**

5¼ ounces ground almonds

2¾ ounces crunchy nut butter of your choice

1¾ ounces coconut oil, melted

3¾ ounces maple syrup

5¼ ounces cornflakes (use gluten-free ones if required)

**For the topping**

½ ounce coconut oil, melted

2½ ounces dried dates (preferably Medjool), pitted and chopped

2½ ounces dried apricots, coarsely chopped

1 tablespoon maple syrup

A pinch of salt

**To decorate**

3½ ounces chopped nuts of your choice

---

### TIP

These nut bars work well with any nut butters or nuts you have in your pantry. We particularly like a peanut version using peanut butter and chopped peanuts.

---

Line a 2-pound loaf pan with baking parchment.

First, make the base. In a food processor, blitz together the ground almonds, nut butter, coconut oil, maple syrup, and cornflakes for a few minutes, until the mixture begins to hold together in a ball.

Press the sandy base mixture into the lined pan and chill in the refrigerator for 20 to 30 minutes.

Meanwhile, make the topping. Place all the topping ingredients with 2 fluid ounces water in the cleaned food processor and blitz until smooth, scraping down the sides in between.

Spread the topping over the top of the chilled base, then sprinkle over the chopped nuts to decorate. Return to the refrigerator for another 30 minutes.

Remove the slab from the pan and slice into 10 thin slices. Store the bars in the refrigerator for up to 5 days.

# Cherry and Coconut Vegan Brownies

Luminary originally started as a wholesale bakery, supplying cafés with cakes and cookies. If you know where to look, you'll still find our bakes for sale in many cafés across London. These brownies are one of our stockists' favorites—loved by vegans and nonvegans alike—and with good reason: they're fudgy and rich, and bursting with juicy cherries and creamy coconut. You wouldn't believe they don't contain butter or eggs! They're perfect with a cup of coffee or warm from the pan.

MAKES 12

4 teaspoons ground flaxseed

10½ ounces all-purpose flour

10½ ounces brown sugar

2¼ ounces unsweetened cocoa powder

1½ ounces dried shredded coconut, plus extra to decorate

½ teaspoon salt

4½ ounces coconut oil

4¼ ounces dark chocolate, broken into pieces

1 tablespoon lemon juice

1 teaspoon vanilla extract

6 fluid ounces coconut milk beverage

7 ounces frozen pitted cherries (fresh are better, just a bit more expensive)

### TIPS

When flaxseeds are ground up and mixed with water, they form a gelatinous liquid that's perfect as an egg replacement and used here to bind the brownies together. You can find them preground in most large grocery stores, usually in the health food section.

Any alternative milk will work in this recipe (almond, oat, soy ...), but we love the added flavor that the coconut one brings.

Preheat the oven to 350°F. Line an 9 x 9-inch baking pan with baking parchment.

In a small bowl, mix together the ground flaxseed and 2 fluid ounces hot water and set aside for about 10 minutes to thicken.

In a large bowl, mix together the flour, sugar, cocoa, dried shredded coconut, and salt until there are no lumps and it's uniform in color.

Melt the coconut oil in a small pan over low heat, then remove from the heat and tip in the chocolate. Stir the chocolate into the oil until all the chocolate is melted and the mixture is silky and smooth. If it hasn't all melted, return it to gentle heat to warm through briefly.

Mix the lemon juice, vanilla extract, coconut milk, and thickened flaxseed mixture into the chocolate-oil mixture.

Make a well in the middle of the dry ingredients, pour in the wet ingredients, and mix until combined.

Spoon the batter into the lined pan and smooth out flat with a spatula.

Dot the top of the batter with the cherries, pressing them in slightly, and dust the top with a little extra shredded coconut.

Bake for 20 to 25 minutes until set but still a little wobbly in the middle. Let them cool completely in the pan before cutting into 12 equal squares.

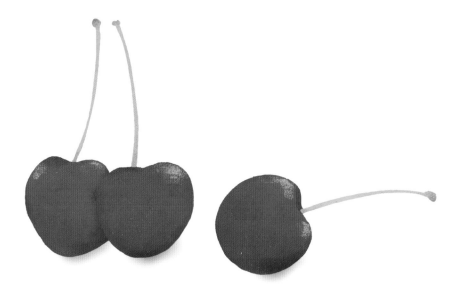

# Lime Leaf Lemon Bars

Kaffir lime leaves are to Southeast Asian cooks what bay leaves are to Western ones—they are often infused in soups, curries, and stews to add background flavor. When finely chopped, they can be used in a similar way to lime zest. We love the more complex zing they bring to the top of our zesty lemon bars!

MAKES 12

**For the shortbread base**
9½ ounces all-purpose flour
2¼ ounces superfine sugar
7 ounces unsalted butter,
  melted

**For the topping**
Zest of 2 lemons
9½ ounces superfine sugar
2¼ ounces all-purpose flour
4 large eggs
3 kaffir lime leaves, stems
  removed, minced
5½ fluid ounces lemon juice
Confectioners' sugar, for
  dusting

Preheat the oven to 375°F and line an 9 x 9-inch baking pan with baking parchment.

First, make the shortbread base. Mix together the flour and sugar in a large bowl, make a well in the middle, and pour in the melted butter. Mix the butter into the flour until a ball of dough forms.

Tip the shortbread dough into the bottom of the lined pan and press down flat, working it into the corners. Prick the shortbread all over with a fork and bake in the oven for 20 minutes until golden around the edges.

While the base is cooking, make the topping. In a separate bowl, rub the lemon zest into the sugar to release its oils. Whisk the flour into the sugar, followed by the eggs and chopped lime leaves, then whisk in the lemon juice.

Remove the pan from the oven and pour the lemony mixture over the shortbread base. Carefully return to the oven for another 15 to 20 minutes. Once baked, it should just have lost its wobble in the middle but it should not be firm to the touch.

Let the bars cool completely in the pan before placing in the refrigerator for 30 to 60 minutes to firm up. Once chilled, cut into 12 equal slices and dust the tops with confectioners' sugar.

SMALL
CAKES

What the cakes in this chapter lack in size, they more than make up for in flavor, texture, and beauty. As these small cakes are individually portioned and decorated, they make perfect picnic or party food—easy to share and more personal than a whole cake.

Muffins make eating cake for
breakfast socially acceptable,
cupcakes take away the stress
of cutting a cake into even slices
plus can be eaten almost anywhere,
and friands and financiers are so
delicate and pretty they'll have
your friends and family cooing
over what you've created.

# MONICA'S STORY

Monica's passionate pursuit of a better life is the definition of tenacity. As a woman who had previously experienced years of violence, she struggled to find the confidence she needed to move forward. And as a single mother, she felt the weight of filling both parental shoes by herself. Despite the odds against her, she fought to regain stability and a better life for her child. After watching a friend graduate from Luminary's program—and seeing its impact on her—Monica knew that she wanted to join the supportive community at the bakery, too.

Although she had always enjoyed cooking, baking remained a bit of an enigma to Monica. However, over the course of Luminary's program, it became a passion—something that brought harmony to her soul. And being with women who believed in her gave her the determination she needed to keep going, even when circumstances were against her. When she broke her ankle, everyone pulled together to help, and she courageously came back and completed the program!

"*Because of my past, I wasn't able to believe in myself. Now, I'm with women who understand my background and who believe in me. The most important thing in life is strength. When you have it, no matter how many ups and downs, you still fight—you see power. That's what I see in Luminary—strength.*"

# Almond Butter and Banana Muffins

When Monica graduated, a version of these banana muffins was part of her application to work at Luminary as an apprentice. We couldn't possibly have turned her—or her delicious baking—down. And so, over time, she mastered the recipe and it took flight. We believe these are everything a banana muffin should be—moist, light, and full of banana flavor. They are, quite simply, *impossible* to say no to!

MAKES 12

3½ ounces whole almonds
5¼ ounces all-purpose flour
1 teaspoon ground cinnamon
1 teaspoon baking powder
1 teaspoon baking soda

¼ teaspoon fine salt
2¾ fluid ounces
    vegetable oil
2¼ ounces dark brown sugar
1 teaspoon vanilla extract
2¼ ounces plain yogurt
2¾ ounces almond butter

1 extra-large egg
14 ounces peeled ripe
    bananas (about 4 medium
    or 3 large bananas)
¾ ounce raw brown sugar

### TIP

To achieve the best flavor in your muffins, use really ripe bananas: bananas so brown and squishy you're unlikely to want to eat them raw will make excellent banana muffins.

Preheat the oven to 350°F and line a 12-cup muffin pan with paper muffin liners.

Spread the almonds out on a baking sheet and toast in the oven for 10 minutes until fragrant. Set aside to cool before coarsely chopping through them a few times to make almond "shards."

Sift the flour, cinnamon, baking powder, baking soda, and salt into a large bowl and mix until completely combined and uniform in color.

In a separate bowl, whisk together the vegetable oil, sugar, vanilla, yogurt, almond butter, and egg until combined.

In a third bowl, mash the bananas until there are only a few small lumps, then whisk the bananas into the wet ingredients.

Make a well in the middle of the dry ingredients and pour the banana mixture into it. Gently stir the wet and dry ingredients together until there is no flour visible. Gently stir in half of the almonds, being careful not to overmix the batter.

Evenly spoon the batter into the paper muffin liners and sprinkle the remaining almonds and raw brown sugar over the top.

Bake for 20 minutes until golden brown and an inserted skewer comes out clean. Let cool in the pan for 10 minutes before transferring to a wire rack to cool completely.

# Sticky Fig Bran Muffins

Our Sticky Fig Bran Muffins are the ultimate mix between fibrous fuel for the day and cake for breakfast. They are sweet but wholesome, sticky but packed with whole grains. They've kept our bakers going on their early morning shifts, and been a favorite postworkout snack for keen runners in our team.

MAKES 12

7 ounces dark brown sugar
3 large eggs
5½ fluid ounces vegetable
    or sunflower oil
8¾ ounces plain yogurt

Grated zest and juice of
    ½ orange
7 ounces bran flakes
5¼ ounces whole wheat flour
1 teaspoon baking powder
1 teaspoon baking soda
½ teaspoon fine salt

1 teaspoon ground cinnamon
½ teaspoon ground ginger
7 ounces dried figs
A handful of rolled oats,
    for sprinkling

Preheat the oven to 325°F and line a 12-cup muffin pan with paper muffin liners.

Combine the sugar, eggs, oil, yogurt, orange zest, and juice in a large bowl and whisk together. Crush the bran flakes between your hands and add to the bowl, mixing to coat them well. Set aside for 10 minutes to soften.

In a separate bowl, sift together the flour, baking powder, baking soda, salt, cinnamon, and ginger and mix to combine.

Cut off and discard the hard stalk from the top of each fig and cut each one into small pieces, about ½ to ¾ inch.

Make a well in the middle of the dry ingredients, pour in the bran mixture, and stir until you have a sloppy muffin batter with no pockets of flour remaining. Tip in the figs and stir them through.

Using an ice-cream scoop or tablespoon, equally spoon the muffin batter between the paper liners—they will be quite full. Sprinkle a handful of oats across the top of each one.

Bake for 25 minutes until well risen and golden brown but still very slightly soft in the middle. Let cool in the pan for 5 minutes before transferring to a wire rack to cool completely.

# KATE'S
# Rye Chocolate Cupcakes with Orange Frosting

In our humble opinion, this is the *only* cupcake recipe you'll ever need. We were a bit speechless when Kate brought these cakes into the bakery a month or two into her internship, and convinced her to share the recipe with us. We've been making them for special occasions ever since, because they really are *very* special.

MAKES 12

For the cupcakes
4½ ounces white rye flour
1 teaspoon baking powder
½ teaspoon baking soda
½ teaspoon fine salt
7 ounces superfine sugar
4½ fluid ounces vegetable oil
5 fluid ounces buttermilk
    (use 3½ ounces yogurt and
    1⅔ fluid ounces milk, if
    you can't find buttermilk)

1 large egg
1 teaspoon vanilla extract
2¼ ounces unsweetened
    cocoa powder

For the orange syrup and
candied peel
½ orange
1¼ ounces honey
Superfine sugar, for
    dredging

For the frosting and garnish
1¾ ounces cream cheese,
    at room temperature
3½ ounces unsalted butter,
    softened
8¾ ounces confectioners'
    sugar
1 teaspoon vanilla extract

Preheat the oven to 350°F and line a 12-cup muffin pan with paper muffin liners or large cupcake liners.

Sift together the flour, baking powder, baking soda, salt, and sugar in a large bowl.

In a separate bowl, whisk together the oil, buttermilk, egg, and vanilla extract.

In a third small bowl, mix together the cocoa and 4 fluid ounces boiling water until it forms a smooth paste. Whisk the chocolate paste into the wet ingredients.

Add the wet ingredients to the dry ingredients and slowly mix to incorporate—the batter will be very runny. Evenly fill each paper liner with the batter, filling each one no more than two-thirds full.

Bake for 15 to 20 minutes until the cakes spring back to the touch and an inserted skewer comes out clean. Let cool in the pan for 10 to 15 minutes before transferring to a wire rack to cool completely.

Meanwhile, make the orange syrup and candied peel. Use a vegetable peeler to pare the orange peel into thin strips of zest, avoiding as much of the white pith as possible. Place the peel in a small pan with the honey and 2⅓ fluid ounces water and set over medium-low heat. Let it simmer for about 15 minutes, stirring occasionally, until you have a pale golden syrup. Strain the syrup from the peel, setting aside both, and let cool to warm.

While still warm, cut the peel into long thin strips and toss in superfine sugar until well coated. Shake off any excess sugar and set the candied peel on a baking sheet to dry.

To make the frosting, place the cream cheese and butter in the bowl of a stand mixer fitted with the paddle attachment. Beat on medium speed for 1 minute until well combined. Add the confectioners' sugar a spoonful at a time, mixing between additions. Once it is all combined, beat the frosting on medium speed for another 1 minute. Add the vanilla and orange syrup and beat again until just mixed in.

To decorate the cupcakes, place an ice-cream scoop of frosting directly in the center of each cake. Take a butter knife and swipe it around the outside edge of the buttercream at a 45-degree angle to the cake, pushing the frosting into a shallow mountain. Next, place the knife in the middle of the mound at a 45-degree angle and turn the cupcake one full turn in the other direction. This should create a nestlike shape of frosting. Decorate the tops with strips of the candied peel.

# Smoky Toffee Apple Cakes

Toffee apples, cinnamon, smoky caramel ... these cakes are like a firework display for your taste buds! Decorated with satisfyingly sour cape gooseberries, their fallen-leaflike casings are ripped open to reveal the bright orange fruit inside. Truly, nothing says fall like these. As soon as fall is over, we're already counting down the months until we can start baking them again ...

MAKES 12

**For the cakes**

4 ounces cold unsalted butter,
   cubed, plus extra for greasing
8 ounces self-rising flour,
   plus extra for dusting
2 teaspoons ground cinnamon
½ teaspoon fine salt
4 ounces dark brown sugar
1 large egg
3½ fluid ounces whole milk
1 tablespoon blackstrap molasses
7 ounces eating apples (2 to 3),
   peeled, cored, and chopped
   into ½-inch pieces
2¾ ounces raisins or golden raisins
12 cape gooseberries, to decorate
   (see tip)

**For the caramel**

1⅔ fluid ounces whole milk
1 lapsang souchong tea bag
1¼ ounces unsalted butter
1 ounce light brown sugar
7 ounces condensed milk

Preheat the oven to 350°F. Grease the cups of a 12-cup muffin pan with butter, making sure to get into every corner and right up the sides, then dust with some flour, tipping it around the whole pan before shaking any excess out.

Sift the flour, ground cinnamon, and salt into a large bowl and mix together. Tip in the cold cubed butter and, using your fingertips, rub the butter into the flour until it looks coarse and sandy, with no large lumps of butter visible. Stir in the dark brown sugar, breaking it up if it's lumpy.

In a separate bowl or jug, whisk together the egg, milk, and blackstrap molasses until combined.

Make a well in the middle of the dry ingredients, pour in the wet ingredients, and mix to form a stiff batter. Add the chopped apples and raisins or

---

### TIP

Cape gooseberries are also known as physalis and are available in most grocery stores. They give a great sharp-sour contrast to the sweetness of the caramel. If you can't find them, slices of fresh fig or blackberries are also lovely here.

---

SMOKY TOFFEE APPLE CAKES

golden raisins to the bowl and mix through until they are just combined.

Evenly distribute the batter between the cups of the prepared muffin pan and smooth flat with the back of a teaspoon. Bake for 15 to 20 minutes until the cakes spring back when lightly pressed and are golden brown.

Let cool in the pan for 5 minutes, then turn the pan upside down on a clean counter and shake a little so the cakes fall from the pan. Place them bottoms up on a wire rack to cool completely.

To make the caramel, add the milk and tea bag to a small pan and bring to a boil. Simmer for 1 minute, then remove and discard the tea bag. Add the butter and light brown sugar to the milk and stir over medium heat until melted and combined. Stir in the condensed milk and bring back to a boil, stirring continuously to keep it from sticking and burning on the bottom of the pan. Keep heating and stirring until the caramel becomes a deep golden brown color. Let cool slightly for 5 minutes.

Carefully spoon the warm caramel over the top of each cake, letting it drip down the sides of each one, then let cool.

Once the caramel has cooled, rip the paperlike cases of the cape gooseberries so that they're fully open and press into the caramel on top of each cake.

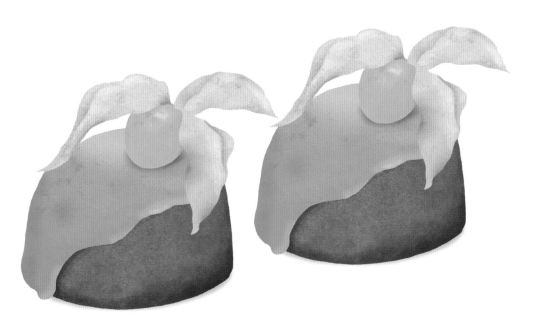

# Lemon and Earl Grey Friands

Delicately aromatic and deliciously fragrant, our lemon friands found their perfect partner in Earl Grey tea. In this original Luminary recipe from years gone by, we use the tea leaves to infuse the butter before baking them into the almond cake batter. The leaves release their subtle flavor and bergamot oils and give the finished friands an attractive speckle.

MAKES 12

For the friands

7 ounces unsalted butter, plus extra for greasing

Gluten-free or all-purpose flour, for dusting

Leaves from 1 Earl Grey tea bag (see tip)

8¾ ounces confectioners' sugar

½ teaspoon fine salt

7 ounces ground almonds

6 large egg whites

Finely grated zest of 1 medium lemon

1 ounce slivered almonds

To decorate

3 tablespoons lemon curd

Dried blue cornflower petals (optional)

Extra Earl Grey tea leaves (optional)

Preheat the oven to 400°F. Grease the cups of a 12-cup muffin pan with butter, making sure to get into every corner and right up the sides, then dust with some flour, tipping it around the whole pan before shaking any excess out.

In a small pan, melt the butter with the tea leaves, then let cool.

Sift the confectioners' sugar, salt, and ground almonds into a bowl and mix together.

In a separate large bowl, use an electric whisk to whisk the egg whites to soft peaks (when you lift the whisk out, it creates peaks in the egg mixture that slowly fall back into the bowl).

Tip the dry ingredients and lemon zest into the bowl of egg whites and gently fold in with a spatula, then pour in the cooled butter and fold in to form a light and bubbly batter.

Equally spoon the friand batter between the cups of the muffin pan and smooth the tops with the back of a teaspoon. Sprinkle the slivered almonds over the top of each one.

Bake for 20 to 25 minutes until the middles are just firm to the touch and the tops are beautifully golden. Let them cool completely in the pan before carefully turning out onto a wire rack or plate.

To decorate, gently warm the lemon curd and 1 tablespoon hot water in the microwave or in a small pan until runny and bubbling. Brush the mixture over the top of each friand and sprinkle with dried blue cornflower petals and a few more tea leaves, if desired.

---

### TIP

Use a tea bag with finely ground leaves o(or grind up loose-leaf tea in a coffee grinder). The tea is mixed into the friand batter, so larger leaves can be woody and unpleasant to eat.

---

# GRACE'S
# Rye, Pear, and Cardamom Financiers with Pistachios

As a child, Grace never had the freedom to explore bakeries, even though she was drawn to them. As time passed, her desire for a career in baking did not subside, but disadvantage began to prevent her life from moving forward. It wasn't until she embarked on an apprenticeship with Luminary that her dream began to come true. After graduating, Grace took a job at a sourdough bakery, immersing herself in the world of grains and spices. Cardamom, in particular, piqued her interest and inspired her to create these delicate cakes, fit for afternoon tea or dessert. Their complex taste and aesthetic beauty are worth the small extra effort they take to make!

MAKES 10

4¼ ounces unsalted butter, cubed, plus extra for greasing
3¼ ounces whole grain or dark rye flour, plus extra for dusting
3 firm Bosc pears
6 cardamom pods, crushed

7¾ ounces confectioners' sugar
1 teaspoon baking powder
½ teaspoon fine salt
2¾ ounces ground almonds
3½ ounces unsalted pistachios, finely chopped, plus additional for sprinkling
7¾ ounces egg whites (about 6 extra-large eggs)

To serve
250g whole crème fraîche
½ teaspoon vanilla extract
25g unsalted pistachios, finely chopped

Preheat the oven to 400°F. Grease 10 cups of a muffin pan with butter, making sure to get into every corner and right up the sides, then dust with some flour, tipping it around the pan before shaking any excess out.

Place the pears on a baking sheet and bake in the oven for 10 to 20 minutes. They should be slightly soft but still firm when squeezed. Once baked, set them aside to cool completely.

Place the butter and cardamom pods in a pan over medium heat. Cook, swirling occasionally, until the butter is browned (see browning butter method on page 108). Set aside to cool slightly.

In a medium bowl, sift together the confectioners' sugar, rye flour, baking powder, salt, and ground almonds. Add the finely chopped pistachios and stir in.

In a separate bowl, gently froth the egg whites with a whisk until bubbles appear and they are loosened. You don't want to whip them or try to make a foam. Add the loosened egg whites to the dry ingredients and mix until smooth.

Strain the butter to remove the cardamom and check the temperature—the butter should be warmer than room temperature but not so hot that it will cook the egg. Pour the strained butter in a stream into the batter, mixing as you do so, until the batter is smooth and glossy. Cover the bowl and chill in the refrigerator for at least 1 hour.

While the batter is resting, quarter and core the cooled pears. Gently cut 4 to 5 thin slices along each quarter, but keep them all attached at the top to make a fan shape. Also, bring the oven back up to temperature.

Once the batter has rested, spoon it into each greased muffin cup, filling them three-quarters full. Gently lay a pear fan over the top of each one (you might need to trim them to fit) and bake in the oven for 20 to 25 minutes until golden and a skewer inserted into the center comes out clean.

To serve, mix the crème fraîche with a little vanilla and gently spoon a dollop onto one side of the top of the cooled financiers. Sprinkle over the chopped pistachios to decorate.

# Black Currant, Lavender, and Mascarpone Cakes

In the days when we had a seasonal cake of the month, this one always belonged to July—the season of black currants and lavender, both flavors evocative of English summertime. Since fresh black currants can be hard to come by (and not everyone has a lavender bush growing nearby), we've made the recipe easy to bake all year round. Tart black currant jam gives purple ripples to the almond sponge and we use dried lavender buds for their delicate perfume.

MAKES 12

**For the cakes**
5¼ ounces unsalted butter, plus extra for greasing
Gluten-free or all-purpose flour, for dusting
5¼ ounces superfine sugar
¾ teaspoon dried lavender buds

3 large eggs
10½ ounces ground almonds
1 teaspoon vanilla extract
3½ ounces black currant jam

**For the mascarpone frosting**
4¼ ounces mascarpone cheese, at room temperature

¾ ounce confectioners' sugar
¼ teaspoon vanilla bean paste

**To decorate**
3 tablespoons black currant jam
A few dried lavender buds

Preheat the oven to 350°F. Grease the cups of a 12-cup muffin pan with butter, making sure to get into every corner and right up the sides, then dust with some flour, tipping it round the whole pan before shaking any excess out.

In a large bowl or with an electric mixer on medium speed, cream together the butter, sugar, and lavender buds for about 5 minutes until fluffy and pale in color. Beat in the eggs, followed by the ground almonds and vanilla extract. Fold the black currant jam through the batter so that it's loosely rippled through but far from a uniform purple color.

Divide the cake batter equally between the cups of the muffin pan, smoothing out the tops with the back of a teaspoon. Bake for 20 minutes, or until an inserted toothpick comes out clean and they are golden brown and firm to the touch.

Let the cakes cool in the pan for 5 minutes before tipping the pan upside down and gently shaking the cakes out onto a wire rack to cool completely. You may need to carefully run a knife around the edge of each cake if they're a little stuck, but avoid this if possible.

To make the mascarpone frosting, mix together the mascarpone cheese and confectioners' sugar, followed by the vanilla bean paste, to give you a smooth, silky, speckled frosting.

Once the cakes are cool, pipe (or spoon, if you don't have a pastry bag) a little "kiss" of the frosting on the top of each upturned cake, slightly off-center, then top with a little spoonful of black currant jam and a small sprinkling of lavender buds.

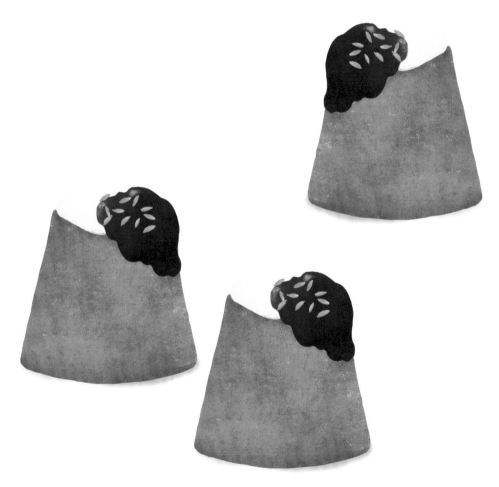

# Honey and Chamomile Cakes

The chamomile tea used in these cakes is made from dried flower heads, so it's delightfully floral and an excellent companion to honey. The cakes are so light and delicate, "fairy cakes" might have been a better name for them!

MAKES 12

For the cakes
2¾ ounces cold unsalted
    butter, cubed, plus extra
    for greasing
6 ounces all-purpose flour,
    plus extra for dusting
7 ounces granulated sugar
1½ teaspoons baking powder
¾ teaspoon baking soda
A pinch of fine salt

Leaves from 2 chamomile tea
    bags (see tip)
5½ fluid ounces whole milk
1 large egg
1 teaspoon vanilla extract

For the syrup
2 tablespoons honey
1 tablespoon boiling water
1 chamomile tea bag

To decorate (optional)
Dried or fresh chamomile
    flowers and finely grated
    lemon zest

### TIP
Use a tea bag with finely ground
leaves (or grind up loose-leaf
tea in a coffee grinder). The tea
is mixed into the cake batter, so
larger leaves can be woody and
unpleasant to eat.

Preheat the oven to 350°F. Grease the cups of a 12-cup muffin pan with butter, making sure to get into every corner and right up the sides, then dust with some flour, tipping it around the whole pan before shaking any excess out.

Sift the flour, sugar, baking powder, baking soda, salt, and the contents of the chamomile tea bags into a large bowl and mix together. Tip in the cold cubed butter and, using your fingertips, rub the butter into the flour until it looks coarse and sandy, with no large lumps of butter visible.

In a separate bowl, whisk together the milk, egg, and vanilla.

Make a well in the middle of the dry ingredients, pour in half of the wet ingredients, and whisk in until just incorporated. Add the second half and continue to whisk until no flour or lumps remain.

Divide the batter between the muffin cups using an ice-cream scoop or large spoon. Bake for 18 to 20 minutes until the cakes spring back when lightly touched.

Let the cakes cool in the pan for 5 minutes before tipping them out onto a wire rack to cool completely.

To make the syrup, mix together the honey, boiling water, and the tea bag in a small bowl and let steep for 5 minutes. Squeeze out the tea bag with the back of a spoon and remove from the syrup.

Prick the top of the cakes all over with a small skewer. Using a teaspoon, spoon the chamomile syrup over the cakes and let it soak in. If desired, decorate each cake with a sprinkling of dried or fresh chamomile flowers and some lemon zest.

# FULL-SIZE
# CAKES

A freshly baked cake is one of the simplest and greatest pleasures in life. They often accompany grand moments of celebration or quiet moments of indulgence. Our bakers take such care to create eye-catching celebration cakes for special occasions and to mark memorable moments. We love to use fresh fruit, herbs, and spices to construct visually stunning centerpieces that reflect the delectable flavors inside each cake. They're (almost) too beautiful to cut into!

But cakes don't always have to accompany a party. Some of our favorites are the kind you'd enjoy making (and then promptly eating) on a drizzly afternoon, just to delight in the process, or to share with friends over a cup of coffee. Cakes, whether you're baking or eating them, provide moments to cherish.

# GISELLE'S STORY

The therapeutic nature of baking cakes can be a pleasure in itself and is something that brought Giselle hope amidst disadvantage.

Life prior to prison was a battle for Giselle. She had been living on the streets and risking everything to make ends meet. When she was released, she was determined to turn her life around. She had so much to live for and didn't want to let another day go by where her circumstances restricted her ambition for a better tomorrow. After being introduced to Luminary by a recruitment consultancy charity working with ex-offenders, she was finally ready to let her ambition loose.

Embracing the Luminary experience opened Giselle's eyes to new opportunities, drawing out skills that were yet to be explored. The art of preparing food for others is strong within Giselle's heritage—with a baker for a grandad and talented cooks for parents, culinary creativity is in her blood. Similarly, being of Jamaican, Malaysian, and Irish descent, she embraces her international origins by bringing together flavors and different traditional cultural dishes from around the world.

Luminary has now become a home for Giselle—a network of women supporting each other.

*"We all feel that the issues we're facing are the biggest or hardest thing we've ever had to deal with. Then, I met some of the amazing women coming through Luminary and it put things into perspective. They've all come from such extraordinary struggles and the most inspirational factor among these women is strength of character and perseverance. They are a constant reminder to me that we are all warriors."*

# GISELLE'S
# Lemon and Poppy Seed Cotton Cake

Inspired by a Japanese vanilla cake, Giselle adapted this recipe so that the clean and light flavor of lemon complements its delicacy. "Heavenly" is the only word to describe it. Whether a simple indulgence or to mark a moment of celebration, this cake aims to please—pair it with a cup of Earl Grey.

## SERVES 8 TO 10

Unsalted butter, for greasing
4 large eggs
3 ounces granulated sugar
1½ teaspoons lemon extract
Finely grated zest of 1 large
    lemon (or 2 small) and
    a squeeze of the juice
2 fluid ounces vegetable oil
2⅓ fluid ounces whole milk
    (or a dairy-free milk,
    such as oat or almond)
4¼ ounces all-purpose flour
1 teaspoon baking powder
1 ounce poppy seeds
Confectioners' sugar, for
    dusting

Preheat the oven to 325°F. Grease and line the bottom and sides of an 8-inch cake pan (not one with a removable bottom) with baking parchment, ensuring the strip around the side reaches at least 2 inches above the top of the pan. Wrap the outside of the pan with foil.

Separate the egg yolks from the whites, placing the yolks in a medium mixing bowl and the egg whites in a large grease-free mixing bowl.

Whisk the egg yolks with half of the sugar until pale and light. Add the lemon extract, lemon zest, oil, and milk and gently stir to combine. Sift the flour and baking powder over the mixture and mix until just combined, being careful not to overmix.

Whisk the egg whites with the squeeze of lemon juice and the remaining sugar until it forms stiff peaks when the beaters are lifted sharply out of the bowl. This should take around 5 minutes with an electric mixer.

Gently fold half of the egg whites and all of the poppy seeds into the batter, then pour the batter into the remaining egg whites, scraping down the sides of the bowl. Gently fold and mix until there are no lumps of egg whites left, being careful not to knock out too much air.

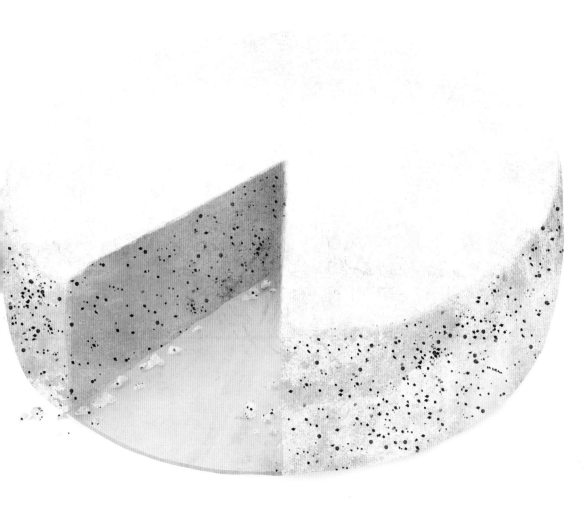

Spoon the batter into the prepared pan and gently spread flat. Place the pan into a water bath (fill a roasting tray with enough boiling water to reach three-quarters of the way up the sides of the pan). Bake for 25 minutes, then turn the oven up to 350°F and bake for a final 10 minutes.

Once baked, carefully remove the pan from its water bath and bang the pan sharply on the counter a couple of times (this will help prevent the cake shrinking). Let the cake cool in the pan for 30 minutes before turning out onto a serving plate.

Lightly dust the top with confectioners' sugar to serve.

# Pear and Saffron Upside-Down Cake

There's something nostalgic and heartwarming about an upside-down cake. A custard-yellow sponge sitting atop—or rather underneath—syrupy pineapple rings. And occasionally, if you're lucky, a couple of candied cherries. It's reminiscent of simpler times, of the seventies, and our grandmas. Our modern version, with saffron and sliced pears, is better suited to a dinner party than sitting around the kitchen table, but contains all the same comforting nostalgia that we often crave.

SERVES 6 TO 8

5¼ ounces unsalted butter,
    softened, plus extra
    for greasing
5¼ ounces superfine sugar
6 saffron threads
15- to 15.25-ounce can pear
    halves
3½ ounces all-purpose flour
1 teaspoon baking powder
½ teaspoon baking soda
A pinch of fine salt
2 large eggs
1 teaspoon vanilla extract
Vanilla ice cream or custard,
    to serve

Preheat the oven to 400°F. Grease and line the bottom of a deep 8-inch cake pan with baking parchment (don't use a pan with a removable bottom, as the syrup will seep out).

Start with the caramel. Place 1¾ ounces of the sugar in a small pan and cook over low heat until it has melted. Don't stir, only swirl the pan until it turns golden brown. Stir in 1¾ ounces of the butter and the saffron threads, then pour into the bottom of the prepared cake pan.

Drain the can of pear halves, setting 3 tablespoons of the juice aside for later. Cut each pear half into slices and neatly arrange them on top of the caramel, overlapping them slightly.

In a small bowl, mix together the flour, baking powder, baking soda and salt.

In a separate bowl, cream together the remaining 3½ ounces each butter and sugar until light and fluffy. Beat the eggs in, one at a time, followed by the vanilla extract, flour mixture, and the reserved canned pear juice. Pour the batter over the top of the pears in the pan.

Bake for 30 to 35 minutes until golden brown on top and the sponge springs back to the touch.

Let cool in the pan for 5 minutes, then loosen the cake from the sides with a knife and turn upside down onto a serving plate. Peel off the parchment and serve warm with ice cream or custard.

# HENRIETTA'S
# Plum and Ginger Pudding Cake

As a Luminary Bakery ambassador, Henrietta Inman has passed her baking knowledge and skills on to many of our trainees, especially with regard to using natural ingredients, seasonal produce, and whole foods. This cake is a great example of what we love about Hen's baking—delicious, beautiful, and full of goodness. Lifted by fresh plums that sink into the moist cake, the whole grain flour and earthy canola oil add an extra depth of flavor and the yogurt makes it super soft, coming together to create that perfect sticky ginger cake that we'll never tire of.

SERVES 8 TO 10

3¾ fluid ounces canola oil, plus extra for greasing
6 ounces whole grain or white spelt flour
½ teaspoon ground cinnamon
3 ounces raw brown sugar
6 ounces molasses sugar (or dark brown sugar)
2 extra-large eggs
3 ounces plain yogurt
3¼ ounces ginger, very finely grated (see tip)
4 teaspoons boiling water
1 teaspoon baking soda
16 ounces plums, halved and pitted

### TIP
For a good ginger flavor you need all the juices and stringy bits that will come from grating the piece of ginger—don't throw any of that away!

Preheat the oven to 325°F. Grease and line the bottom of a deep 8-inch cake pan with baking parchment (don't use a pan with a removable bottom as the batter is quite runny and will leak out).

In a large bowl, sift together the flour and ground cinnamon to get rid of any lumps.

In a separate bowl, use a whisk to thoroughly mix together the canola oil, sugars, eggs, yogurt, and ginger.

Make a well in the center of the flour mixture, pour in the wet ingredients, and gradually mix it in to form a runny batter.

In a separate bowl or pitcher, combine the boiling water with the baking soda. Add this to the mixture, folding it in gently, until everything is well combined and there are no more pockets of flour visible.

Pour the batter into the prepared pan. Arrange the plum halves on top, overlapping them if necessary and letting them sink into the batter.

Bake for 65 to 75 minutes, turning the pan around in the oven halfway through. The cake is ready when the top springs back to the touch and a skewer inserted into the center comes out with a just few crumbs clinging to it.

Let cool in the pan for 30 minutes, then remove from the pan and enjoy when it's still a little warm. The cake will keep well in the refrigerator for up to 5 days.

# Raspberry and Red Currant Buttermilk Layer Cake

We like to think of berries as the jewels of the natural world and love how they adorn this layer cake like a crown. The tartness of the buttermilk, raspberries, and red currants in the pillowy sponge offsets the sweetness of the buttercream and brings a beautiful pop of color with every slice. Reminiscent of a beloved Victoria Sponge, it really is a cake fit for royalty— or that someone special in your life!

SERVES 10 TO 12

**For the cake**
12 ounces unsalted butter, softened, plus extra for greasing
14¾ ounces all-purpose flour, plus extra for dusting
1 teaspoon fine salt
1 teaspoon baking powder
1 teaspoon baking soda
14 ounces superfine sugar
3 large eggs, plus 2 egg whites
2 teaspoons vanilla extract
7 fluid ounces buttermilk (or mix 2 fluid ounces milk with 5 ounces yogurt)
5¼ ounces fresh raspberries
5¼ ounces fresh red currants

**For the buttercream**
10½ ounces unsalted butter, softened
22 ounces confectioners' sugar
3¾ fluid ounces buttermilk (alternatively, mix ¾ fluid ounce whole milk with 1¾ ounces yogurt)
1 teaspoon vanilla extract
A pinch of fine salt

**For the filling**
3½ ounces raspberry jam
3½ ounces red currant jelly

**To decorate (optional)**
Freeze-dried raspberry powder or pieces
Fresh raspberries
Fresh red currants
Coconut shavings
Dried rose petals
Pomegranate seeds
Sprigs of fresh rosemary

Preheat the oven to 350°F. Grease and line three 8-inch cake pans with baking parchment. Dust the greased edges of the pans with a little flour, tapping out any excess.

Sift the flour, salt, baking powder, and baking soda into a bowl and mix together.

In a separate large bowl, use an electric mixer to cream together the butter and superfine sugar until light and fluffy. Beat in the eggs, egg whites, and vanilla extract (it will look a little separated, but don't worry—it will come back together once the flour has been added). Gently mix in the flour, followed by the buttermilk and mix until there are no lumps left.

Fold the raspberries and red currants into the batter and evenly spoon it into the cake pans, smoothing the tops out with a spatula. Bake in the oven for 25 to 30 minutes until the sponges spring back to the touch and an inserted skewer comes out clean.

Let the sponges cool in the pans for 5 minutes, before turning out onto wire racks to cool completely.

Meanwhile, make the buttercream. In a large bowl, beat the butter until soft, then gradually add half of the confectioners' sugar, a spoonful at a time, beating it in between each addition. Mix in the buttermilk, vanilla, and salt, then beat in the other half of the confectioners' sugar.

In another small bowl, stir together the raspberry jam and red currant jelly to loosen and combine them.

When the sponges are completely cool, trim the domed tops off with a bread knife to make them flat. Set aside the cake you trimmed off and crumble it onto a baking sheet. Bake the cake crumbs in the oven at 350°F for 5 to 10 minutes until crisp.

Place a cake board or serving plate on a turntable or counter (see tip on page 163) and smear a little buttercream on the top. This buttercream will act as glue and stop the cake from sliding around. Peel off the baking parchment from the sponge layers and place the first sponge layer, cut side up, on the cake board or plate. Spread a quarter of the buttercream on the top of the sponge, going right to the edge. Leave an indent in the middle of the buttercream and fill it with half of the jam filling, spreading it to about ¾ inch away from the edge of the cake.

Place a second sponge layer on top of the buttercream, cut side down. Spread another quarter of the buttercream on the top of this second layer, pushing it just over the edge, followed by the remaining jam filling.

Place the third sponge layer on top, cut side down. Spread another quarter of the buttercream on the top of this layer, pushing it just over the edge.

Spread the final quarter of the buttercream around the sides of the cake, until the whole cake is covered in an even layer of buttercream and any gaps are filled. Place a bench scraper at a 90-degree angle against the side of the cake (see tip, below) and turn the turntable (or your plate) to smooth the sides flat and create a patchy or "naked" look to the frosting on the sides of the cake. (Don't worry if you push some buttercream onto the top of the cake.)

To finish the cake with a smooth 90-degree angle on the top, use a palette knife to neatly drag the top edge of buttercream into the middle of the cake.

To decorate, mark out a Luminary crescent moon shape on the top of the cake using freeze-dried raspberry powder, tapering off the ends—this will be your guide for the rest of the toppings. Place chunks of the baked cake crumble at intervals around the crescent shape, with the largest pieces at the widest section of the moon and smaller pieces toward the ends. Repeat with the raspberries and red currants, draping them across the top. Finally, place the coconut pieces, rose petals, pomegranate seeds, and rosemary sprigs in among the fruit, spacing them evenly and keeping the ends of the moon shape tapered.

### TIP

At Luminary, we use a few of bits of equipment only keen cake makers usually own: a turntable, a small palette knife, and a bench scraper. They make getting a perfectly smooth finish on a cake a lot easier and are well worth the investment if you decorate cakes regularly. If you don't have these to hand, instead of a turntable, you can place the cake on a large, flat plate and rotate it on your counter. A butter knife and spatula are enough instead of a palette knife. And don't worry about the bench scraper—you'll be fine without!

# Spiced Squash Layer Cake with Cream Cheese Frosting

This recipe reminds us of the seasons changing, as the leaves turn from green to gold and a new chill is found in the air. The smell of roasting squash and pumpkin spice in this cake will rise from the oven and fill your kitchen as you bake, in a glorious celebration of harvesttime. Topped with fluffy cream cheese frosting and a sprinkling of pumpkin seeds, it's hard to imagine a better way to celebrate fall!

SERVES 10 TO 12

For the cake
1 butternut squash (26 ounces prepeeled weight)
Unsalted butter, for greasing
16 ounces self-rising flour, plus extra for dusting
10½ ounces brown sugar
4¼ ounces blackstrap molasses
1¾ ounces plain yogurt
8 fluid ounces vegetable oil
1 teaspoon vanilla extract
4 large eggs
½ teaspoon fine salt
1 teaspoon baking soda
2 teaspoons ground ginger
2 teaspoons ground cinnamon
1 teaspoon ground nutmeg

For the frosting
7 ounces unsalted butter, softened
3½ ounces cream cheese, at room temperature
10½ ounces confectioners' sugar
1 teaspoon vanilla extract

To decorate (optional)
¼ teaspoon ground cinnamon
5 to 6 cape gooseberries
Sprigs of fresh rosemary
Pumpkin seeds
Unsalted pistachios, shelled

Preheat the oven to 350°F and line a baking sheet with baking parchment.

Cut the butternut squash in half, scoop out the seeds, and score the flesh, going as deep as the skin. Place the halves upside down on the prepared sheet, cover with foil, and bake for 1 hour until soft to the tip of a knife. Let cool, uncovered.

Meanwhile, grease and line the bottom of three 8-inch cake pans with baking parchment. Dust the greased inside edges of the pans with a little flour, tapping out any excess.

In a large bowl, whisk together the brown sugar, blackstrap molasses, yogurt, oil, vanilla, and eggs until well combined.

Peel the skin off the cooled squash and weigh out 16 ounces of the flesh. Mash until smooth with a potato masher or whiz in a blender to a puree. Scrape the squash puree into the egg mixture and whisk in. Sift the flour, salt, baking soda, and ground spices over the mixture and fold in until no lumps remain.

Evenly pour the batter into the prepared pans, then bake for 20 to 25 minutes until the sponges spring back to the touch and an inserted skewer comes out clean.

Let the sponges cool in the pans for 5 minutes before turning out onto a wire rack to cool completely.

Meanwhile, make the frosting. In a large bowl, beat the butter and cream cheese together until fluffy and glossy. Gradually beat in the confectioners' sugar, a spoonful at a time, followed by the vanilla.

When the sponges are completely cool, trim the domed tops off with a bread knife to make them flat. Set aside the cake you trimmed off and crumble it onto a baking sheet. Bake the cake crumbs in the oven at 350°F for 5 to 10 minutes until crisp.

Place a cake board or serving plate on a turntable or counter (see tip on page 163) and smear a little frosting on the top. This frosting will act as glue and stop the cake from sliding around. Peel off the baking parchment from the sponge layers and place the first sponge layer, cut side up, on the cake board or plate. Spread a quarter of the frosting on the top of the sponge, pushing it just over the edge.

Place a second sponge layer on top of the frosting, cut side down. Spread another quarter of the frosting on the top of this second layer, pushing it just over the edge.

SPICED SQUASH LAYER CAKE WITH CREAM CHEESE FROSTING

Place the third sponge layer on top, cut side down. Spread another quarter of the frosting on the top of this layer, pushing it just over the edge.

Spread the final quarter of the frosting around the sides of the cake, until the whole cake is covered in an even layer of frosting and any gaps are filled. Place a bench scraper at a 90-degree angle against the side of the cake (see tip on page 163) and turn the turntable (or your plate) to smooth the sides flat and create a patchy or "naked" look to the frosting on the sides of the cake. (Don't worry if you push some buttercream onto the top of the cake.)

To finish the cake with a smooth 90-degree angle on the top, use a palette knife to neatly drag the top edge of frosting into the middle of the cake.

To decorate, mark out a Luminary crescent moon shape on the top of the cake using ground cinnamon, tapering off the ends—this will be your guide for the rest of the toppings. Place chunks of the baked cake crumble at intervals around the crescent shape, with the largest pieces at the widest section of the moon and smaller pieces toward the ends. Repeat with the cape gooseberries (with their papery cases torn open like flower petals to reveal the jewel-like fruit inside) and the rosemary sprigs, spacing them evenly and keeping the ends of the moon shape tapered. Finally, sprinkle over the pumpkin seeds and pistachios to fill any gaps.

# JESS'S
# Banoffee Birthday Cake

Jess, one of our interns, is always bubbling with enthusiasm—ready to celebrate even the smallest of life's achievements. She would bake you a cake for practically anything: finishing your book, remembering to walk the dog, making the perfect cup of tea ... Her cakes are, in essence, a celebration, so if there ever was the most perfect way to mark another year of *you*, it would be her Banoffee Birthday Cake. The sweet, buttery cookie base adds a great crunch, which contrasts with the soft banana sponge and velvety salted caramel buttercream—the queen of desserts, in a cake.

SERVES 10 TO 12

For the cookie base
7½ ounces graham crackers
    (roughly 14 crackers)
3¾ ounces unsalted butter
1¾ ounces light corn syrup

For the banana sponge
13¼ ounces unsalted butter,
    softened, plus extra
    for greasing
13¼ ounces self-rising flour,
    plus extra for dusting
13¼ ounces brown sugar

6 large eggs
½ teaspoon ground
    cinnamon
6 really ripe bananas
    (about 19¼ ounces)
2 teaspoons vanilla extract

For the salted caramel
buttercream
8¾ ounces unsalted butter,
    softened
18 ounces confectioners'
    sugar
7 ounces ready-made
    caramel or dulce de leche
1 teaspoon kosher or sea salt

To decorate
¼ teaspoon ground
    cinnamon
2 to 3 graham crackers,
    broken into pieces
Honeycomb or cinder
    toffee pieces
Banana chips
Walnuts, hazelnuts, or
    pecans
Chocolate chips or buttons
Extra ready-made caramel
    or dulce de leche

Preheat the oven to 350°F. Grease and line the bottom of three 8-inch pans with baking parchment. Dust the greased edges of the pans with a little flour, tapping out any excess.

Start with the cookie base. Put the graham crackers into a sealable plastic food bag and use a rolling pin to crush them until there are no big chunks of cracker left.

Gently melt the butter in the microwave or in a small pan over low heat and stir into the cracker mixture, along with the light corn syrup. Mix together until the mixture resembles wet sand and sticks together well.

Tip the cookie mixture into one of the lined pans and firmly press it down with the back of a spoon to create an even cookie base—it's really important to form a solid base for the cake, to prevent it crumbling when it comes out of the pan. Place in the refrigerator for 20 minutes to set firm.

Next, make the banana sponge. In a large bowl, cream the butter and sugar together using a spatula or an electric mixer until pale, light, and fluffy. Slowly mix in the eggs, one at a time, until fully incorporated, then add the flour and cinnamon and gently fold in using a spatula or spoon.

Mash the bananas using a fork or potato masher and gently mix into the cake batter.

Spoon the batter into the pans, filling them about two-thirds full, and spread them level with a spatula. The pan with the cookie base should have slightly less mixture in than the other two, so that they're all the same height.

Bake for 25 to 30 minutes until the sponge is springy to the touch and an inserted skewer comes out clean. Leave in the pans until completely cool.

Meanwhile, make the buttercream. In a large bowl, beat the butter using a spatula or electric mixer until it is slightly lighter in color. Add the confectioners' sugar, a spoonful at a time, mixing between each addition until it's all incorporated (this will give you a smooth buttercream and avoid too much mess). Stir in the caramel and salt and mix to a creamy consistency.

BANOFFEE BIRTHDAY CAKE

When the sponges are completely cool, carefully turn them out of the pans. The cookie base may break a little at the edges, but don't worry—it should stay bonded to the sponge. Trim the domed tops off the sponges with a bread knife to make them flat.

Place a cake board or serving plate on a turntable or counter (see tip on page 163) and smear a little buttercream on the top. This buttercream will act as glue and stop the cake from sliding around. Peel off the baking parchment from the sponge layers and place the cookie/sponge layer, sponge side up, on the cake board or plate. Spread a quarter of the buttercream on the top, pushing it just over the edge.

Place a second sponge layer on top of the buttercream, cut side down. Spread another quarter of the buttercream on the top of this second layer, pushing it just over the edge.

Place the third sponge layer on top, cut side down. Spread another quarter of the buttercream on the top of this layer, pushing it just over the edge.

Spread the final quarter of the buttercream around the sides of the cake, until the whole cake is covered in an even layer of buttercream and any gaps are filled. Place a bench scraper at a 90-degree angle against the side of the cake (see tip on page 163) and turn the turntable (or your plate) to smooth the sides flat and create a patchy or "naked" look to the buttercream on the sides of the cake. (Don't worry if you push some buttercream onto the top of the cake.)

To finish the cake with a smooth 90-degree angle on the top, use a palette knife to neatly drag the top edge of buttercream into the middle of the cake.

To decorate, mark out a Luminary crescent moon shape on the top of the cake using the ground cinnamon, tapering off the ends—this will be your guide for the rest of the toppings. Place chunks of the the graham crackers at intervals around the crescent shape, with the largest pieces at the widest section of the moon and smaller pieces toward the ends. Repeat with the honeycomb pieces and then the banana chips, spacing them evenly and keeping the ends of the moon shape tapered. Use the nuts and chocolate chips to fill in any spaces. Finally, drop or pipe small splodges of caramel into any remaining gaps.

# SARAH'S STORY

Sarah came to Luminary after discovering baking as a form of therapy while she struggled with a diagnosis of Post Traumatic Stress Disorder. Her Pistachio, Blackberry, and White Chocolate Layer Cake (see page 174) is significant, as it was one of the first creations she made when she discovered baking. By the end of the whole process, she was covered in confectioners' sugar and the kitchen was in disarray, but the smiles on her guests' faces as they tucked into slice after slice said it all. That was the moment that changed everything for Sarah, and her passion for baking took her on a whole new journey.

As a Luminary graduate, staff member, and now business owner (see page 255), Sarah has been unstoppable in sharing her story of recovery and using it as encouragement for others.

*"I started baking to help get out of my own head. Even if it was just for five seconds, I finally had a moment of peace ... The most important thing someone told me, when I was at the hardest point in my journey, was that 'Sometimes we have to break down in order to break through!' My dad was the one who said that to me and I remember thinking, 'That's what I'm going to do.' It gave me hope that this is not the end—there's hope for me!"*

# SARAH'S

# Pistachio, Blackberry, and White Chocolate Layer Cake

Sarah's cake is a delicious way to bring people together, which she can attest to after a neighbor's daughter showed up at her home to learn this sweetly layered recipe. Whether it's broadening your baking horizons or you're savoring each bite of it at a party, this cake suitably weds the pop of fresh blackberry with the light pistachio sponge, making it perfect for any celebration!

SERVES 10 TO 12

For the cake
11¾ ounces unsalted butter,
    softened, plus extra
    for greasing
11¾ ounces self-rising flour,
    plus extra for dusting
7¾ ounces superfine sugar
6 large eggs
3½ fluid ounces whole milk
1 teaspoon vanilla extract
3½ ounces unsalted
    pistachios, finely chopped
3½ ounces fresh (or frozen)
    blackberries

For the buttercream
5¼ ounces white chocolate,
    broken into pieces
5¼ ounces unsalted butter,
    softened
8¾ ounces confectioners'
    sugar
½ teaspoon vanilla extract

To decorate
Unsalted pistachios
    (a mixture of whole
    and finely chopped)
Fresh blackberries (some
    whole, some cut in half)
White chocolate buttons
Sprigs of fresh rosemary
Fresh mint leaves
Pomegranate seeds

Preheat the oven to 350°F. Grease and line the bottom of three 8-inch pans with baking parchment. Dust the greased edges of the pans with a little flour, tapping out any excess.

In a large bowl, cream the butter and sugar together with an electric mixer until light and fluffy. Mix in the eggs, one at a time, until fully incorporated. Mix in half of the flour, then half of the milk, mixing until no floury or milky patches remain, before adding the remaining flour and milk. Mixing on low speed, add the vanilla extract and pistachios until incorporated.

Carefully fold the blackberries into the batter by hand, to avoid the mixture turning an unappetizing blue-gray color from the juices they can release.

Divide the batter evenly between the lined pans. Bake for 20 to 25 minutes until the sponges spring back to the touch and an inserted skewer comes out clean.

Let cool in the pans for 10 minutes before gently turning the sponges out onto a wire rack to cool completely.

To make the buttercream, melt the white chocolate by placing it in a bowl set over boiling water (don't let the bottom of the bowl touch the water). Alternatively, gently melt it in the microwave, being careful to stop and stir it every 30 seconds to avoid burning it.

In a large bowl, beat the butter for 1 to 2 minutes, then gradually add the confectioners' sugar, a spoonful at a time, mixing it in before adding the next. Once all of the confectioners' sugar is incorporated, mix in the vanilla and melted white chocolate.

When the sponges are completely cool, trim the domed tops off with a bread knife to make them flat.

Place a cake board or serving plate on a turntable or counter (see tip on page 163) and smear a little buttercream on the top. This buttercream will act as glue and stop the cake from sliding around. Peel off the baking parchment from the sponge layers and place the first sponge layer, cut side up, on the cake board or plate. Spread a quarter of the buttercream on the top of the sponge, pushing it just over the edge.

Place a second sponge layer on top of the buttercream, cut side down. Spread another quarter of the buttercream on the top of this layer, pushing it just over the edge.

Place the third sponge layer on top, cut side down. Spread another quarter of the buttercream on the top, pushing it just over the edge.

Spread the final quarter of the buttercream around the sides of the cake, until the whole cake is covered in an even layer of buttercream and any gaps are filled. Place a bench scraper at a 90-degree angle against the side of the cake and turn the turntable (or your plate) to smooth the sides flat and create a patchy or "naked" look to the buttercream on the sides of the cake. (Don't worry if you push some buttercream onto the top of the cake.)

To finish the cake with a smooth 90-degree angle on the top, use a palette knife to neatly drag the top edge of buttercream into the middle of the cake.

Decorate the top of the cake with a Luminary crescent moon shape using all of the decoration ingredients. First, sprinkle the finely chopped pistachios into a moon shape, tapering off the ends—this will be your guide for the rest of the toppings. Place the blackberries in the shape, with the whole ones at the widest section of the moon and the smaller pieces toward the ends. Repeat with the whole pistachios and white chocolate buttons. Finish by placing small sprigs of rosemary and mint leaves in among the fruit and use more chocolate buttons and pomegranate seeds to fill in any gaps.

# LAURA'S
# Lemon and Thyme Drizzle Loaf

Lovely Laura's Lemon Loaf (try saying that a few times!) is a crowd-pleaser that will never let you down, much like our lovely baker Laura. Full of zesty lemon and hints of thyme, this springlike and jolly cake looks beautiful, drizzled in bright white frosting and decorated with sprigs of thyme.

**SERVES 8 TO 10**

**For the cake**

7 ounces unsalted butter,
    softened, plus extra
    for greasing
7 ounces superfine sugar
4 large eggs
A handful of fresh thyme
    (about ¼ ounce on the
    stem), leaves picked, plus
    extra sprigs to decorate
7 ounces all-purpose flour
2 teaspoons baking
    powder
A pinch of fine salt
Finely grated zest
    of 2 lemons

**For the frosting**

10½ ounces confectioners'
    sugar
1⅓ fluid ounces lemon juice

Preheat the oven to 350°F. Grease and line a 2-pound loaf pan (8½ x 4½ x 2½ inches) with 2 strips of baking parchment overlapping on the bottom of the pan to line each side.

In a large bowl, cream together the butter and sugar for a couple of minutes until light and fluffy. Add the eggs to the mixture, one at a time, thoroughly beating each one in before adding the next.

In a separate bowl, mix the thyme leaves with the flour, baking powder, salt, and lemon zest. Add to the butter mixture and fold in until no floury patches remain.

Spoon the batter into the prepared pan, spreading it level with a spatula. Bake for 40 to 45 minutes until an inserted skewer comes out clean. Let the cake cool in the pan for 10 minutes before transferring to a wire rack.

Meanwhile, make a thick frosting by mixing together the confectioners' sugar and lemon juice.

While the cake is still warm, poke about 20 holes in the top using a skewer. Gently spoon the frosting evenly over the top of the cake, letting it run down the sides in thick ribbons. Decorate with a few fresh thyme sprigs laid over the wet frosting. Let cool completely so the frosting sets before cutting into slices.

# Blood Orange Polenta Loaf

We consider a good gluten-free polenta cake a staple in any baker's repertoire, but a worthy alternative to a lemon polenta cake can be hard to come by. Blood oranges are so colorful and have a lovely balance between sweet and sharp—their bright pinky-orange juice livens up the syrup soaked into this cake. Their stunning coloring it is also a fun surprise every time they are cut open. If you want to make this cake outside blood orange season, you can substitute regular oranges.

SERVES 8

For the cake
6¾ ounces unsalted butter,
    softened, plus extra
    for greasing
6¾ ounces light brown sugar
Finely grated zest and juice
    of 2 blood oranges
    (about 5 fluid ounces)
3 large eggs
4¼ fluid ounces fine
    cornmeal (the finer the
    better)
7 ounces ground almonds
½ teaspoon baking soda
½ teaspoon baking powder
A pinch of fine salt
5¼ ounces plain yogurt
5¼ ounces superfine sugar

To decorate (optional)
5¼ ounces superfine sugar
1 blood orange, cut into
    ⅛ to ¼-inch slices

Preheat the oven to 350°F. Grease and line a 2-pound loaf pan (8½ x 4½ x 2½ inches) with 2 strips of baking parchment, arranged in a cross shape overlapping on the bottom of the pan to line each side.

In a large bowl, use an electric mixer to cream together the softened butter, light brown sugar, and orange zest until light, fluffy, and paler in color. Beat in the eggs, one at a time, scraping down the sides with a spatula as necessary, until all the eggs are incorporated (don't worry if it looks as though it has separated—once you add the almonds in, it'll come back together).

In a separate bowl, mix together the cornmeal, ground almonds, baking soda, baking powder, and salt.

Sift the cornmeal and almond mixture into the butter mixture and mix until everything is well combined (use an electric mixer on medium speed if you have one), then add the yogurt and mix until well combined.

Spoon the batter into the prepared loaf pan and spread flat. Bake for 40 to 45 minutes until golden brown and a knife or skewer inserted into the center of the cake comes out clean.

Meanwhile, make the syrup. Combine the orange juice and superfine sugar in a small pan and bring to a boil, stirring every now and again. Simmer for another 3 minutes and then remove from the heat and let cool in the pan.

Once the cake has finished baking, pierce the loaf about 15 to 20 times with a skewer, making sure to go right the way through the cake to the bottom of the pan. Pour all of the syrup over the cake and let soak in the pan until cooled.

If decorating with candied orange slices, combine 7 fluid ounces water and the sugar in a pan over medium heat and stir and swirl until all the sugar is dissolved and you're left with a translucent syrup. Tip the orange slices into the syrup and bring to a boil, then reduce the heat, cover the pan with a lid, and cook on low simmer for about 40 minutes.

Remove the pan from the heat and let cool with the lid on. When cool, take the orange slices out of the syrup and arrange on top of the cake to decorate.

## TIP

Syrup soaks best into a cake if either the syrup is hot and the cake cold, or the syrup is cold and the cake hot. In this recipe, we pour cold syrup over a hot cake, but if you need to let the cake cool before you can make the syrup, make sure the syrup is steaming hot before pouring it over.

# Coffee and Cardamom Cake with Pumpkin-Seed Brittle

Coffee has many good companions—chocolate, caramel, walnuts—but in this cake we think we might just have found our favorite: cardamom. Its spicy warmth complements the coffee's toasty bitterness rather than overshadowing it and allows both flavors to shine together.

**SERVES 8 TO 10**

**For the cake**
5¾ ounces unsalted butter, softened, plus extra for greasing
5¾ ounces self-rising flour, plus extra for dusting
4¾ ounces light brown sugar
1½ ounces light corn syrup
½ teaspoon vanilla extract
3 large eggs
Seeds from 6 cardamom pods, crushed to a fine powder with a mortar and pestle
½ teaspoon baking powder
2 tablespoons instant coffee granules
2 tablespoons boiling water

**For the buttercream**
2¾ ounces unsalted butter, softened
5¼ ounces confectioners' sugar
1 tablespoon instant coffee granules

**To decorate**
1¾ ounces pumpkin seeds
3½ ounces granulated sugar
1 teaspoon unsweetened cocoa powder

Preheat the oven to 350°F. Grease and line a deep 8-inch cake pan with baking parchment. Dust the greased edges of the pan with a little flour, tapping out any excess. Additionally, line a baking sheet with a sheet of baking parchment.

In a large bowl, use an electric mixer to cream together the butter, brown sugar, and light corn syrup until pale and fluffy. Beat in the vanilla and eggs until well combined (it may separate a little, but don't worry—it'll come back together when you add the flour). Mix the flour, ground cardamom seeds, and baking powder into the batter.

In a separate, small bowl, mix together the instant coffee and boiling water, then stir into the batter.

Spoon the batter into the lined pan and smooth out with a spatula. Bake for 30 to 35 minutes until the sponge springs back to the touch and an inserted skewer comes out clean. Let cool in the pan for 5 minutes before tipping out onto a wire rack to cool completely.

To make the buttercream, whisk up the softened butter with an electric mixer and spoon in the confectioners' sugar, a little at a time, until well combined and the mixture is fluffy.

In a separate bowl, make a paste with the coffee granules and 1 tablespoon boiling water and cool before whipping it into the buttercream.

To make the pumpkin-seed brittle, toast the pumpkin seeds in a dry skillet over low heat, shaking the pan now and again, until they've all popped and puffed up. Tip them out in a single layer onto the lined baking sheet.

Put the granulated sugar into a small pan and let it melt over medium heat, swirling the pan, but never stirring, until it has turned a copper color. Pour the caramel over the pumpkin seeds and let cool and set hard. This will take 5 to 10 minutes. When the brittle is set rock hard, snap it into shards.

Ensure the cake is completely cool before starting to decorate.

Dollop the buttercream in a mound on top of the sponge and use
a palette or butter knife to push it out to the very edges of the cake
and create rough waves of buttercream. Lightly dust the top of the
buttercream with a little unsweetened cocoa powder and arrange
the brittle shards on the top.

PASTRY

Due to pastry's temperament and some pretense around it, our Luminary trainees often find the prospect of making pastry daunting. But with a little guidance and a lot of "just having a go," it doesn't take them long to realize that it's not as hard as they first thought! It's usually at this moment they also realize how far they've come, how much they've learned, and that, like most things in baking, by faithfully following a recipe, they can create something impressive.

Pastry is flexible by nature, swaying with ease between lusciously sweet and deliciously savory. It also has many characteristics, from soft and pillowy, to crumbly and short, to flaky and crisp, each variety as wonderful as the next and as varied as the women we train. Our graduates hope that by challenging yourself to make a new pastry, you too will find the same sense of accomplishment and pride as they have.

# ANNA'S STORY

Anna* is always our go-to for pastry! With her eye for detail and an Albanian upbringing that meant she mastered the intricate delicacy of pastry from an early age, we're forever grateful to her for introducing us to her impressive Spinach Byrek (recipe on page 192).

Anna made her very first byrek at the age of twelve. After watching her mom make them for years, it was finally her turn. She remembers the challenge of stretching the dough to an exquisitely fine layer and how the scent of white onions filled the whole house. It all came together for the end result of delicious and perfectly flaky byrek.

As the years passed, Anna experienced some painful, life-changing times—and eventually decided to move to the UK for a fresh start. She began to seek out ways to work and support her child, but the doors remained firmly closed. Following a recommendation from a support worker, she discovered Luminary Bakery, and we're so glad that she did!

*Name changed to protect identity

"I wanted to learn, because when I came to this country I didn't know a lot, not even English. But I wanted to change our lives for the better. In life, you meet people who make all the difference. Before I came on the course, I didn't know what I wanted to do. I had two hands and a child to look after, but nothing was happening. Then I met Alice [Luminary's Founder] and she said, 'You want something. Let's make it happen together!' That was the motivation I needed. After coming to Luminary, I started to accept that maybe I could do it. And now, I dream!"

# ANNA'S
# Spinach Byrek

A customer favorite at our cafés, *byrek* are delicious Albanian flaky pastries stuffed with a savory filling. Anna's family recipe is at the heart of this version, but with her own added twist: a spinach and feta filling with cracked black pepper on top. The light, savory flavors sandwiched between layers of buttery pastry are perfect at any time of the day, whether you're hard at work or dreaming up dreams.

MAKES 6 TO 8

**For the pastry dough**
10½ ounces high-gluten
  bread flour
1 teaspoon fine salt
1 tablespoon sunflower
  or vegetable oil

**For the filling and assembly**
2¾ ounces **ghee**, melted
  (see tip)
4 teaspoons sunflower
  or vegetable oil
10½ ounces fresh spinach
10½ ounces feta or crumbly
  sheep cheese
Salt and cracked black pepper

Start with making the dough. Mix together the flour and salt in a large bowl, then make a well in the middle and tip in 7½ fluid ounces warm water and the oil. Use a wooden spoon or bench scraper to bring it together into a dough, eventually kneading it together with your hands.

Tip the dough out onto a clean counter and knead it for 10 minutes until it's really stretchy and elastic. Put the dough back into the bowl, cover with plastic wrap or a damp dish towel, and let rest for 1 hour.

Meanwhile, make the filling. Combine 1 ounce of the ghee and the oil in a large pan over medium heat. Add the spinach and gently cook down until wilted and most of the moisture has been cooked off. Remove the pan from the heat and stir in the crumbled cheese. Taste the mixture and season with salt and pepper to taste.

Preheat the oven to 375°F and grease the bottom and sides of an 9 x 9-inch baking pan with melted ghee.

Lightly flour a clean counter and rolling pin. Turn the dough out of the bowl and cut it into 6 equal pieces. Taking one piece at a time, roll and stretch each one out as thin as you can using the rolling pin and your hands—the dough should be thin enough to read newspaper print through it. If it starts to stick, lift it up and dust more flour underneath.

Cut the dough into rectangles the same size as your pan. Collect any scraps so you can reroll them and make as many sheets as you can.

Layer a third of the pastry rectangles in the pan, brushing each one with some of the remaining melted ghee before laying the next one on top. Spoon half of the spinach filling on top of the pastry stack and spread it out to make an even layer.

Layer the next third of the pastry rectangles on top of the spinach, again brushing with melted ghee between each layer. Top with the second half of the spinach filling and spread it out flat.

Layer the final third of the pastry on top, brushing melted ghee between each layer as before. Brush the very top layer with the last of the ghee and sprinkle with cracked black pepper.

Bake for 30 to 35 minutes until deep golden brown on top. Let cool, then remove from the pan, and cut into 6 to 8 large squares.

**TIP**

Ghee is clarified butter and can be found in most large grocery stores, usually in the Asian food section. If you can't find any, then ordinary salted butter will work fine!

# Feta, Caramelized Red Onion, and Thyme Quiche

In week sixteen of our bakery training program, we teach our trainees to make shortcrust pie dough—and, with it, our infamous quiche. Some have never heard of quiche before, some only have memories of eating soggy beige pie dough, but very few have ever experienced a proper homemade, deep-filled quiche as it should be. Plentiful red onions and feta sit over a crumbly whole wheat dough, suspended in a silky, just-cooked egg filling. This quiche has gained converts both in and out of our classroom.

SERVES 4 TO 6

### For the pie dough

5¼ ounces whole wheat all-purpose flour, plus extra for dusting

A pinch of fine salt

2¾ ounces cold unsalted butter, cubed

### For the filling

¾ ounce unsalted butter

2 red onions, thinly sliced

Fine salt

1 tablespoon brown sugar

1 tablespoon balsamic vinegar

4 large eggs

10 fluid ounces heavy cream

1⅔ fluid ounces whole milk

1 tablespoon fresh thyme leaves, plus extra to garnish

Pepper, to taste

5¼ ounces feta cheese

First, make the pie dough. Combine the flour and salt in a bowl and rub the butter in with your fingertips until it resembles bread crumbs. Sprinkle over 3 tablespoons cold water and bring together into a ball of dough. If it doesn't come together easily, add a little more water. Wrap the dough in plastic wrap and let rest in the refrigerator for 30 minutes.

To make the filling, melt the butter in a large nonstick skillet over medium heat. Add the onions with a pinch of salt and cook for 20 minutes until soft, stirring occasionally. Stir in the sugar and vinegar and cook over low heat for 5 minutes until the mixture is sticky. Set aside to cool.

Meanwhile, preheat the oven to 350°F.

Roll out the chilled dough on a floured counter to about 1/16 inch thick, rotating it now and then to avoid sticking. Lift the pastry into an 8-inch pie dish, gently lifting and tucking it to line the sides and bottom of the dish. Leave a little overhang of dough around the edges.

Line the pie shell with baking parchment, fill with pie weights or uncooked rice/lentils, and bake for 15 to 20 minutes. (This weighs the dough down while it bakes, ensuring it remains flat and even, and is called "blind baking.") After this time, remove the beans/rice and the baking parchment and return the pie shell to the oven to bake for another 10 minutes, or until the base feels dry, looks cooked, and has no oily patches. Gently trim the excess dough from around the edge of the pan with a small serrated knife.

Whisk together the eggs, cream, milk, thyme leaves, and **a good pinch each** of salt and pepper.

Fill the base of the pie shell with the sticky onions, crumble the feta over the top, then pour over the creamy egg mixture.

Gently transfer the quiche to the oven and bake for 30 to 35 minutes until golden brown on the top and there is only a small wobble in the center.

Sprinkle a few more thyme leaves on top and let cool a little before serving warm. Alternatively, cool completely, then refrigerate before cutting into neat slices.

# DOUBRA'S STORY

Doubra's first experience of baking took place after reclaiming a baking book that was due to be thrown away. The methodical process of baking became a stress reliever as she began to create beautiful and luscious treats—starting from simple single-cup bakes and moving on to cakes. This growing enjoyment became a stabilizer during her time living at a London hostel.

With an ambition to grow in her newfound skill and embrace its therapeutic qualities, she kept an eye out for opportunities and eventually was accepted onto Luminary's Employability Training Program.

Doubra was initially hesitant. Everything was new and the extra effort it took to leave the house and travel across London seemed like a lot of pressure. But, after a while, she became determined to push through!

Even during the breadmaking sessions—a class she was not particularly fond of—she motivated herself through all the kneading and frustrations to not only complete the class but graduate from our program.

*"They teach you, even if you feel like you cannot do it or you want to quit. They'll help you see that you're worth more than just letting a little incident ruin things."*

# DOUBRA'S
# Nigerian Chicken Sausage Rolls

Doubra's sausage rolls pack a punch and will bring instant vibrancy to any picnic basket or packed lunch! The delicious pastry packages are not only a fusion of Doubra's Nigerian roots and a favorite British classic, but are also testament to her own perseverance. While taking part in Luminary's program, there were times that she wanted to give up, but her incredible determination meant she always carried on—in the end, she was unstoppable!

MAKES 16

**For the pastry**

18 ounces all-purpose flour, plus extra for dusting
¼ teaspoon fine salt
8¾ ounces cold butter, cut into ½-inch cubes

**For the filling and assembly**

2 Scotch bonnet chiles
1 chicken bouillon cube
1 ounce piece of ginger, peeled
6 garlic cloves, peeled

28¼ ounces chicken sausages, casings removed
2 teaspoons ground nutmeg
1½ teaspoons cayenne pepper
1 teaspoon dried thyme
1 large egg, beaten

Start with the dough. Combine the flour, salt, and butter in a large bowl and shake to coat the butter in the flour. Add 8 to 9 fluid ounces water, 4 tablespoons at a time, mixing it in with a butter knife to begin with, then using your hands to bring it together into a slightly sticky, butter-dotted dough.

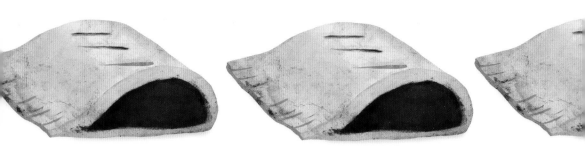

Tip the dough onto a floured counter and roll out to a large rectangle, 38 x 12 inches. With the short sides of the dough facing you, fold the top short edge down toward you, just past the center of the dough, then fold the bottom third up over it to make a rectangle a third the size of the original. Rotate the rectangle by 90 degrees and repeat the rolling and folding process another 2 times. Wrap the dough in plastic wrap and chill in the refrigerator until the filling is ready.

Preheat the oven to 350°F and line a baking sheet with baking parchment.

To make the filling, whiz the chiles, bouillon cube, ginger, and garlic in a small food processor to a smooth paste (or cut them up as finely as possible). In a bowl, combine the paste with the chicken sausage, nutmeg, cayenne pepper, and dried thyme and mix until well combined.

Cut the chilled dough in half and place one half back in the refrigerator. Roll out on a lightly counter to a 38 x 12-inch rectangle, about ¹⁄₁₆ inch thick. Take half of the filling mixture and arrange in a long log down the middle of the full length of the dough rectangle. Leave a ¾-inch gap along one of the long edges. Brush the ¾-inch strip of dough with the beaten egg and fold the other long edge of the dough over the top of the sausage to enclose it. Use a fork to crimp the edges together to form a seal. Cut the roll into 8 pieces and place them on the lined baking sheet. Brush the tops with more egg wash and use a sharp knife to score a couple of lines in the top of each one.

Repeat the process with the other half of the dough and filling mixture to make another 8 sausage rolls.

Bake in the oven for 35 to 40 minutes until golden brown all over.

Let cool for 10 minutes before tucking in, as they'll be piping hot in the middle.

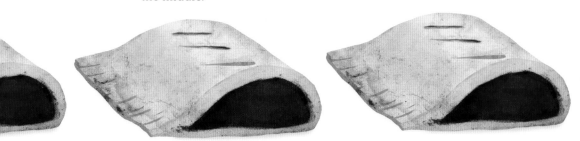

# BENJAMINA'S
# Apple, Sage, and Honey Frangipane Tart

Luminary ambassador Benjamina Ebuehi is a wonderful teacher, faithful supporter, and inspiration to many of our trainees. Just like an older sister, she has imparted plenty of her recipes, tips, and tricks, including how to make her stunning apple pies. We love the way she marries savory sage with caramelized apples in this tempting tart covered in honeyed frangipane, all neatly contained within her melt-in-the-mouth pie dough.

### SERVES 8 TO 10

**For the pie dough**

9¾ ounces all-purpose flour, plus extra for dusting

3½ ounces confectioners' sugar

A pinch of fine salt

5¾ ounces cold unsalted butter, cubed

1 large egg plus 1 egg yolk, beaten together

**For the apple and sage sauce**

3 Granny Smith apples, peeled, cored, and coarsely chopped

2 teaspoons lemon juice

1 tablespoon finely chopped fresh sage leaves

1 tablespoon superfine sugar

**For the frangipane and apple filling**

8 ounces unsalted butter, softened

8 ounces superfine sugar

2¼ ounces honey

1 teaspoon vanilla extract

3 large eggs

8 ounces ground almonds

2 tablespoons all-purpose flour

A pinch of fine salt

2 Granny Smith apples

Handful of slivered almonds

**To decorate**

10 to 15 small sage leaves

Confectioners' sugar, for dusting

Honey, for drizzling

To make the pie dough, combine the flour, sugar, and salt in a large bowl, add 3 tablespoons cold butter, and use your fingertips to rub it into the flour until the mixture resembles coarse bread crumbs.

Make a well in the center of the flour, pour in the eggs, and use a knife to stir and bring the dough together.

Turn the dough out onto a clean counter and very gently knead it for up to 10 seconds until smooth and soft. Wrap in plastic wrap and let it rest in the refrigerator for 45 minutes.

Unwrap the chilled dough and place on a lightly floured counter. Roll the dough out to about ⅛ inch thick, giving it a quarter turn every so often to avoid it sticking.

Line a 9-inch round tart pan (preferably with a removable bottom) with the dough, letting it overhang the edge of the pan by just over ½ inch. Place it in the freezer for 15 minutes to firm up.

Preheat the oven to 400°F.

APPLE, SAGE, AND HONEY FRANGIPANE TART

To make the apple and sage sauce, put all the ingredients into a small pan, and cook over low heat for 12 to 15 minutes until the apples are softened. Remove from the heat and mash the apples with a fork or potato masher to get a thick sauce. Set aside to cool completely.

To make the frangipane, beat the butter, superfine sugar, honey, and vanilla together using a stand mixer or electric mixer for 3 to 5 minutes until pale and creamy. Add the eggs, one at a time, beating well after each addition. Stir in the ground almonds, flour, and salt and beat briefly to combine.

Put the frangipane batter into a large disposable pastry bag and snip off the end. Set aside.

Remove the dough from the freezer and use a sharp knife to trim off the overhanging dough. Spoon the apple sauce evenly over the base of the dough, then pipe the frangipane on top. Use a palette knife or spatula to smooth out the top.

Core the apples but leave the skins on, cut them into quarters, then thinly slice. Arrange the apple slices on top of the frangipane, letting them overlap slightly. Sprinkle the slivered almonds over the top.

Bake for 45 to 55 minutes until the pastry is golden and the frangipane is set. If the tart gets too dark before it's completely cooked, cover it with a sheet of foil and continue to bake.

Remove the tart from the oven and let cool completely before removing it from the pan. Top with the sage leaves, dust with confectioners' sugar, and serve with a drizzle of honey.

# Strawberry, Rhubarb, and Tarragon Turnovers

Tarragon is a herb that's often banished to savory dishes, but its unique anise flavor makes it the perfect addition to our strawberry and rhubarb turnovers. We love how its bitterness balances the sweetness of our lively strawberry and rhubarb compote in these little handheld pastries.

MAKES 10

**For the pie dough**
8¾ ounces all-purpose flour, plus extra for dusting
⅛ teaspoon fine salt
1½ teaspoons superfine sugar
4½ ounces cold unsalted butter, cut into ½-inch cubes

**For the compote filling**
3¾ ounces strawberries, stems removed, sliced

8 ounces rhubarb, cut into ¾-inch slices
2¾ ounces superfine sugar
1 teaspoon cornstarch
½ teaspoon finely chopped fresh tarragon
1 egg, beaten, to glaze
Raw brown sugar, for sprinkling

Start with the pie dough. Combine the flour, salt, sugar, and butter in a large bowl and shake to coat the butter in the flour. Add 8 to 9 tablespoons water, a couple of tablespoons at a time, mixing it in with a blunt knife to begin with, then bringing it together with your hands to make a slightly sticky, butter-dotted dough. If it's still dry and flaky, add a little more water.

Tip the dough onto a floured counter and roll out to a large rectangle, 38 x 12 inches. With the short sides of the dough facing you, fold the top short edge down toward you, just past the center of the dough, then fold the bottom third up over it to make a rectangle a third the size of the original. Rotate the rectangle by 90 degrees and repeat the rolling and folding process another 2 times. Wrap the dough in plastic wrap and chill in the refrigerator for at least 1 hour.

Meanwhile, make the filling. Combine the strawberries, rhubarb, and superfine sugar with 1 tablespoon of water in a medium pan over low heat. Gently cook the fruit for 15 minutes, stirring occasionally, until the juices have been released and it's starting to break down.

Mix the cornstarch with 2 tablespoons of water to make a paste. Pour this into the stewed fruit and mix in well. Continue to cook for 5 minutes, then stir in the chopped tarragon and set aside to cool.

Preheat the oven to 350°F and line a baking sheet with baking parchment.

Roll out the dough on a lightly floured counter to a 20 x 8-inch rectangle, about 1/16 inch thick. Trim the edges of the dough to make them straight, then cut the dough into 10 even squares.

Place 1 tablespoon of the fruit compote in the center of each dough square, leaving a border clear around the edges. Brush the edges with beaten egg and fold one corner of each dough over to meet the opposite corner to make a triangle, encasing the compote and sealing the edges.

Transfer the turnovers to the lined sheet, brush the tops with more beaten egg, and make a small cut in the top of each one to let any steam escape. Sprinkle the tops with raw brown sugar and bake for 30 to 35 minutes until golden brown.

# ABBY'S
# Blackberry and Thyme Tart

Abby, a founding baker at Luminary, was inspired by the day her friend and fellow baker Sarah took her out to forage for wild blackberries near our first bakery. Enchanted by the berries' rare appearance, the result was this delicious, colorful tart. As Sarah was vegan and Abby on a refined-sugar- and gluten-free diet, this was something they could both enjoy and a great use for the treasures of their trip.

SERVES 8 TO 10

**For the dough**
3¾ ounces coconut oil
1 teaspoon finely chopped fresh thyme leaves
1¾ ounces coconut sugar
¼ teaspoon fine salt
¾ ounce banana, mashed

6 ounces gluten-free all-purpose flour

**For the blackberry filling**
12 ounces fresh blackberries
8 tablespoons maple syrup
1¾ ounces cashews, soaked for 2 to 4 hours or overnight, then drained

2 tablespoons maple syrup
A pinch of fine salt
½ teaspoon agar agar powder (or 2 teaspoons vege-gel)
4 tablespoons coconut oil

**To decorate**
6 ounces blackberries
A few sprigs of fresh thyme

To make the dough, melt the coconut oil in a small pan over low heat. Once melted, remove from the heat and stir in the chopped thyme. Let the mixture cool and infuse for about 20 minutes.

In a bowl, whisk the cool thyme-infused oil with the coconut sugar, salt, and banana until the mixture no longer separates. If it won't come together, put it in the refrigerator and check every 3 to 5 minutes until it is cool enough to hold together when whisked and looks creamy. Mix in the flour until a dough forms.

Quickly press the dough into the bottom and sides of a 9-inch tart pan (preferably one with a removable bottom), focusing on making the edges as even as possible. Poke several holes with a fork over the surface of the dough, then place in the freezer for 30 minutes.

Meanwhile, preheat the oven to 325°F.

Put the tart pan on a baking sheet, line with baking parchment, and fill with pie weights or uncooked rice/lentils. Bake blind for 10 minutes (see page 195), then remove the parchment and beans/rice and bake for another 15 to 20 minutes until the base feels dry, looks cooked, and has no oily patches.

Transfer the pan to a wire rack and let cool completely.

To make the blackberry filling, combine the blackberries and 6 tablespoons of the maple syrup in a small pan and bring to a boil over medium heat. Reduce the heat, cover the pan, and simmer for 20 minutes. Stir every now and again until the berries have released their juices.

Pour the mixture into a blender or food processor and blend to a vibrant puree, then press through a fine strainer to remove the seeds. Weigh out 8¾ ounces of the puree and set aside to use in the filling, then chill the remaining puree until ready to serve.

Put the blackberry puree, soaked and drained cashews, maple syrup, and salt into the blender/food processor and process until completely smooth. Leave in the blender while you prepare the agar agar and coconut oil.

In a small pan, combine 4¼ fluid ounces water with the agar agar and bring to a boil, then continue to boil for another 2 to 3 minutes, whisking continuously until it dissolves. At the same time, melt the coconut oil in a separate pan.

As soon as the agar mixture is ready, with the motor of the blender running, carefully pour the hot agar mixture into the blender, gradually increasing the speed from low to high, then blending at high speed for 30 seconds. Repeat this process with the melted coconut oil, making sure it's fully incorporated before stopping.

Pour the filling into the cooled tart shell. Very carefully, gently tap the tart on the counter to release any air bubbles. Cut a portion of baking parchment large enough to cover the surface of the tart and delicately smooth the paper directly onto the surface of the filling. Chill in the refrigerator for at least 2 hours.

When chilled, remove the tart from the pan and very slowly peel off the parchment, beginning at one side and peeling to the other. Decorate the top of the tart with the blackberries and a few sprigs of thyme and serve with the remaining chilled blackberry puree.

# Soda Bread Treacle Tart

At Luminary, we're passionate about soda bread and its versatility (see recipes on pages 66, 68, and 76). It's always best eaten fresh on the day it's baked, but if we do have any left over, we love creating recipes to use it up. This recipe was developed with that in mind, giving soda bread scraps a new lease on life in this sticky, sweet treacle tart.

SERVES 8 TO 10

**For the pie dough**
7 ounces all-purpose flour,
    plus extra for dusting
1¾ ounces whole wheat flour
¼ teaspoon fine salt
5¼ ounces cold unsalted
    butter, cubed
1 large egg, beaten

For the filling
25 ounces light corn syrup
Finely grated zest of
    ½ lemon
1½ tablespoons lemon juice
2 large eggs
1⅔ fluid ounces heavy cream
¼ teaspoon fine salt
7 ounces stale soda bread,
    crusts trimmed off

To serve
Whipped cream or
    crème fraîche

First, make the dough. In a large bowl, mix together the flours and salt and tip in the cubed butter. Rub the butter into the flour with your fingertips until it resembles bread crumbs. Make a well in the middle of the mixture and add the egg, then use a butter knife and then your hands to work it into a **ball**. Add a little cold water if it's still dry and flaky. Flatten the ball of pastry into a thick disk and wrap in plastic wrap. Chill in the refrigerator for 30 to 60 minutes.

Roll out the chilled dough on a lightly floured counter to a circle, about 11 to 12 inches in diameter and ¼ inch thick. Rotate the dough and flour the counter as needed, to prevent the dough sticking.

Gently transfer the dough to an 8-inch round tart pan (about 1¼ inches deep and preferably with a removable bottom), gently lifting and tucking it into the edges of the pan to line it all the way around. Use a sharp knife to trim the overhanging dough in line with the edge of the pan. Place the pan on a baking sheet and chill in the refrigerator for 30 minutes.

Meanwhile, preheat the oven to 350°F.

Line the pie shell with a large piece of baking parchment and fill with pie weights or uncooked rice/lentils, right up to the top of the pan. Bake blind for 25 minutes (see page 195), then remove the parchment and beans/rice and bake for another 5 minutes, or until it looks dry with no oily patches and is starting to turn golden.

Meanwhile, make the filling. In a large bowl, whisk together the syrup, zest and lemon juice, eggs, cream, and salt until smooth.

Pulse the bread in a food processor or grate on the large holes of a box grater to turn it into bread crumbs.

Sprinkle the bread crumbs into the eggy mixture and mix a few times to cover the crumbs in the mixture. Go gently—overmixing will make a tough, heavy filling.

**Once the pie shell is baked,** pour in the filling, ensuring it's evenly distributed. Bake for 45 to 50 minutes until golden brown and the middle is just about set with no wobble.

Cool in the pan for 10 minutes before gently lifting out to serve with whipped cream or crème fraîche.

# Greengage and Elderflower Bakewell Tart

Greengages are a sweet and golden-green variety of plum that make excellent preserves. The sticky jam tastes similar to rhubarb or gooseberry—slightly tart and fruity. It perfectly lends itself to this floral take on a classic, complementing the sweet and mellow elderflower and almonds in the sponge. Divine!

**SERVES 8 TO 10**

**For the pie dough**
7 ounces all-purpose flour, plus extra for dusting
2 tablespoons confectioners' sugar
¼ teaspoon fine salt
3½ ounces cold unsalted butter, cubed
1 large egg, beaten

**For the frangipane**
4½ ounces unsalted butter, softened
Finely grated zest of ½ lemon
3½ ounces superfine sugar
3 large eggs
2 tablespoons elderflower cordial
5¼ ounces ground almonds
2 tablespoons all-purpose flour
6 tablespoons greengage jam (see tip)
1 ounce slivered almonds
Yogurt, to serve (optional)

## TIP
Greengage jam is available in most large grocery stores, but if you can't find it, try rhubarb, gooseberry, or even black currant jam. The tart will be a little different but still delicious!

First, make the pie dough. In a large bowl, mix together the flour, confectioners' sugar, and salt and tip in the cubed butter. Rub the butter into the flour with your fingertips until you have a mixture like bread crumbs. Make a well in the middle of the mixture and add the egg, then use a butter knife and then your hands to work it into a ball. Add a little cold water if it's still dry and flaky.

Flatten the ball of dough into a thick disk and wrap in plastic wrap. Chill in the refrigerator for 30 to 60 minutes.

Roll out the chilled dough on a lightly floured counter to a circle, about 11 to 12 inches in diameter and ¼ inch thick. Rotate the dough and flour the counter as needed, to prevent it sticking.

Gently transfer the dough to an 8-inch round tart pan (about 1¼ inches deep and preferably one with a removable bottom), gently lifting and tucking it into the edges of the pan to line it all the way around. Use a sharp knife to trim the overhanging dough in line with the edge of the pan. Place the pan on a baking sheet and chill in the refrigerator for 30 minutes.

Meanwhile, preheat the oven to 350°F.

Line the pie shell with a large piece of baking parchment and fill with pie weights or uncooked rice/lentils, right up to the top of the pan. Bake blind for 20 minutes (see page 195), then remove the parchment and beans/rice and bake for another 5 minutes, or until it looks dry with no oily patches and is starting to turn golden. **Transfer the pan to a wire rack and let cool completely.**

Meanwhile, make the frangipane. Cream together the butter, lemon zest, and sugar with an electric mixer on medium speed until pale and aerated. Beat in the eggs, one at a time, followed by the elderflower cordial. Gently mix in the ground almonds and flour until they're incorporated.

Spread the jam across the bottom of the cooled pie shell. Dollop the frangipane on top in 5 large blobs and spread flat with a spatula. Sprinkle over the slivered almonds. Bake for 35 to 40 minutes until the frangipane springs back to the touch when lightly pressed.

Let cool completely, then remove from the pan. Serve with yogurt, if desired.

# Peach and Raspberry Gal-ettes

Our "gal-ettes" were originally made to celebrate International Women's Day, in honor of all of the "gal pals" and wonder women in our community and across the globe. These individual free-form tarts are crafted from buttery shortcrust pastry filled with fresh peaches and raspberries. Both sweet and tart, juicy and crumbly, this recipe acts as a reminder that balance is important and celebrates working toward a more gender-balanced world.

MAKES 12

**For the pie dough**

11¼ ounces all-purpose flour,
   plus extra for dusting
1 tablespoon brown sugar
½ teaspoon fine salt
8 ounces frozen **butter**

**For the filling**

4 peaches, halved, pitted,
   and cut into ¼-inch slices
8¾ ounces raspberries
2 teaspoons cornstarch
2 teaspoons raw brown
   sugar, plus extra for
   sprinkling
1 large **egg**, beaten,
   to glaze

To make the dough, mix together the flour, sugar, and salt in a large bowl. Use a box grater to grate the frozen butter into the flour and briefly rub it in until the pieces are the size of oats and well coated in the flour. Make a well in the middle of the mixture and add 6 tablespoons of cold water, using a butter knife or bench scraper to mix it together into a dough. If it's really dry and flaky, mix in an extra 2 to 3 tablespoons of water. Bring the dough into a disk shape, wrap in plastic wrap, and let rest in the refrigerator for at least 1 hour.

Meanwhile, make the filling. Put the peach slices and raspberries into a bowl and gently toss in the cornstarch and sugar to coat the fruit.

Preheat the oven to 400°F. Line a couple of baking sheets with baking parchment.

Unwrap the chilled dough and place on a lightly floured counter. Roll out the dough until it is ¼ inch thick. Using a bowl or small plate as a guide, cut out

5-inch circles from the dough and transfer them to the lined baking sheets. Evenly arrange the fruit in the center of each pastry circle, leaving at least 1 inch clear around the edges. Fold, pleat, and seal the edges of the dough over the edges of the filling, leaving the middles exposed. Brush the edges of the dough with beaten egg and sprinkle with a little extra sugar.

Reduce the oven temperature to 350°F, then immediately place the gal-ettes into the oven to bake for 30 to 35 minutes until the pastry is golden brown and the fruit is bubbling.

Let cool a little before serving.

# DESSERTS

Dessert, pudding, afters, a *sweet* ... whatever you call it, we're *those* people—pudding people! We'll take or leave an appetizer, but for us a meal's not finished until dessert has been served and spoons licked clean. Dessert speaks of hospitality, care, and generosity. It prolongs a meal, providing space to savor time together and enjoy conversation and connection. It might be as small as a piece of fruit or a dollop of yogurt, but if the opportunity arises we love to embrace desserts in all their glory and really make a show of it. At Luminary, we're also people people—thriving in these moments of gathering and community. We can't think of anything worse than being stuck in the kitchen, slaving over a highly complicated and intricate showstopper while our guests are having fun ... without us. For this reason we've pulled together the recipes in this chapter to be delicious, but also straightforward and stress-free, so you can spend precious time with those you love. The perfect ending to a meal!

# TANYA'S STORY

Although contentment was a rarity in her childhood home, happy memories of being in the kitchen with her mother have been reassuring to Tanya when life hasn't been so kind.

After a traumatic attack in which Tanya barely escaped with her life, she became more determined than ever to seek restoration for her life. She found a Jamaican recipe for banana fritters (see page 220), among many others, to be therapeutic during her recovery. She courageously began to volunteer with charities who were helping other women from domestic violence backgrounds and began exploring business opportunities that would give her independence.

With Tanya's ambition to start her own business growing, she was introduced to Luminary. Over the period of the course and observing the resilience of the other women she met, she was inspired! Tanya was able to draw out the talent and skills that were already rising within herself.

Today, cooking and baking has become a means for Tanya to inspire hope in those who have undergone similar life-changing experiences to her own. Whether it's sharing freshly baked goods or learning how to create them, food has a significant way of bringing people together. Tanya's tip, whether you're new to baking or a true veteran, is:

*"Always cook with love."*

"Even before I arrived, I got a sense that Luminary believed in me. They want you to do well! Their way of working inspires you to do well. They give you hope. They really empower women to be their best selves."

# TANYA'S
# Banana Fritters with Cinnamon Sugar

The delectability of Tanya's banana fritters leaves no room for debate. With their vibrancy rooted in Jamaican culture, your senses are destined to awaken as soon as the oil gets hot! This was one of the first Jamaican recipes Tanya learned and she has fond memories of being in the kitchen with her mother as the irresistible aromas of sweet banana and cinnamon sugar filled the room.

SERVES 4
(MAKES ABOUT 16)

For the fritters
11¾ ounces peeled bananas
   (about 3 bananas)
⅛ teaspoon freshly grated
   nutmeg
½ teaspoon ground
   cinnamon

1 teaspoon vanilla extract
1½ ounces light brown
   sugar
5¾ ounces all-purpose flour
½ teaspoon baking powder
A pinch of fine salt
4 tablespoons vegetable or
   sunflower oil, or more
   as needed, for frying

For the cinnamon
sugar
4¼ ounces superfine sugar
1 teaspoon ground cinnamon

To serve
Yogurt or vanilla ice cream
   (dairy free, if you like)

In a medium bowl, mash the bananas until they are creamy with just a few small chunks left. Stir in the nutmeg, cinnamon, vanilla, 4 tablespoons water, and light brown sugar until combined. Sift the flour, baking powder, and salt over the mixture and mix in until you have a thick batter.

Make the cinnamon sugar by stirring together the superfine sugar and cinnamon in a shallow bowl and set nearby.

Heat the oil in a large nonstick skillet over medium heat. To test when it's hot enough for frying, add a small dollop of the batter to the oil and watch for it to sizzle and brown. When it's hot enough, carefully drop tablespoons of the banana batter into the pan, swirling the oil over them as they spread out. It's best to fry no more than 5 to 6 fritters at a time so you don't overcrowd the pan. Fry for 3 to 4 minutes on each side until the fritters are a dark golden brown. Lift them out of the pan with a slotted spoon and drain on paper towels for 30 seconds.

Add a little more oil to the pan, if needed, and repeat until all the batter is used up.

Tip the still-hot fritters into the cinnamon sugar and turn to coat on every side. Serve immediately, still warm from the pan, with a dollop of yogurt or a scoop of vanilla ice cream.

# Apricot and English Breakfast Tea Clafoutis

We can't think of a lovelier way to round off a dinner party than with our cheery, just-warm, apricot-studded clafoutis. You're aiming to bake the clafoutis until there's just a little wobble left in the middle and the edges are puffed and golden—somewhere between a baked custard and a flan. It's also ideal for those who like to get ahead. You can make the batter up to a day in advance and leave it in the refrigerator until you're ready to bake. Just pour the batter into the dish and pop the clafoutis in the oven as you're sitting down to start the meal. It'll be ready as soon as you are!

## SERVES 6

11¼ ounces ripe apricots

2½ ounces superfine sugar

2 tablespoons Cointreau

9½ fluid ounces whole milk

1 English breakfast tea bag

¾ ounce unsalted butter,
   melted, plus extra for
   greasing

1½ ounces raw brown sugar

1¾ ounces all-purpose flour

A pinch of fine salt

2 large eggs

Finely grated zest of
   ½ orange

Confectioners' sugar,
   for dusting

Slice the apricots in half down their creases and twist to remove the pits and separate the halves. Place the halves in a bowl with 1 ounce of the superfine sugar and the Cointreau and stir together, bashing the apricots a little with a spoon. Cover the bowl and let soften for a minimum of 30 minutes, but ideally for a couple of hours or overnight.

Bring the milk to a simmer in a small pan over medium heat. As soon as it comes to a simmer, turn off the heat and stir in the tea bag and butter until it is melted. Let cool and infuse.

Preheat the oven to 400°F and grease the bottom and sides of an 8-inch baking dish with a little butter. Tip the raw brown sugar into the greased dish, then shake the dish from side to side to cover the bottom and sides with a sugary coating.

Add the remaining 1½ ounces of superfine sugar, the flour, and salt to a large bowl and mix together. Make a well in the middle, crack in the

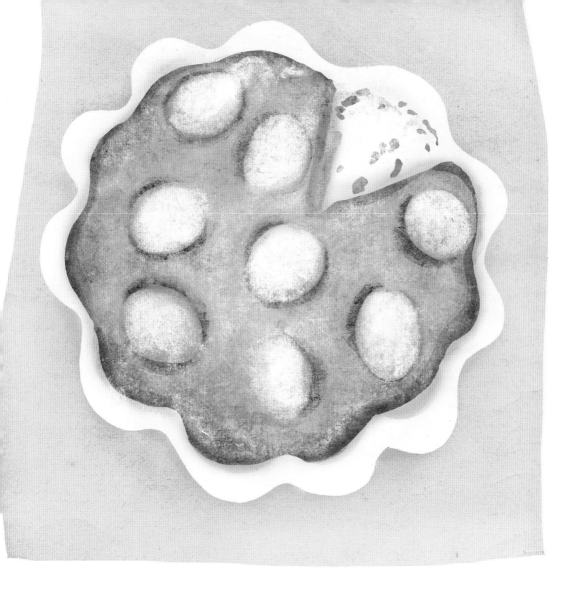

eggs, and whisk to combine. Strain in the cooled milk mixture, add the orange zest, and whisk until there are no lumps remaining.

Arrange the apricot halves in the bottom of the sugared dish.

Pour any remaining apricot juices into the batter mixture and whisk in.

Pour the batter over the apricots and bake for 30 to 35 minutes until the clafoutis is set to the touch but still has a bit of a "wobble" in the middle.

Let cool for 10 minutes, then dust with confectioners' sugar and serve warm.

# SUSIE'S

# Cardamom and Orange Butterscotch Pudding

Susie used to work as a baker onboard a ship, which made her a dab hand in the galleylike kitchen in Luminary's second premises. Although she kept us afloat on harder days with her humor and silly stories, we always knew she meant business. This sticky cardamom pudding, smothered in silky orange butterscotch sauce, is no exception!

SERVES 8

For the cardamom pudding

3¾ ounces unsalted butter, softened, plus extra for greasing

Finely grated zest and juice of 1 orange

8¾ ounces dried dates (preferably Medjool), pitted and chopped

6 ounces dark brown sugar

4 large eggs

Seeds from 10 green cardamom pods, crushed as finely as possible with a mortar and pestle

8 ounces all-purpose flour

1 teaspoon baking powder

1 teaspoon baking soda

For the orange butterscotch sauce

3½ ounces superfine sugar

7 fluid ounces heavy cream

2 fluid ounces freshly squeezed orange juice

½ teaspoon kosher or sea salt

5¼ ounces unsalted butter, at room temperature

To serve (optional)
Crème fraîche

Preheat the oven to 325°F and grease and line an 8-inch square baking pan with baking parchment.

Combine the zest and orange juice along with the dates in a small pan and bring to a simmer over medium to low heat. Continue to simmer for 5 to 10 minutes until the dates are soft.

Transfer the dates and juice to a food processor and blitz to a smooth paste, then set aside to cool.

Using an electric mixer, cream the butter and brown sugar together until soft, light, and fluffy. Crack in the eggs, one at a time, beating between each addition, followed by the cooled date paste and mix until combined. Sift the ground cardamom seeds, flour, baking powder, and baking soda over the mixture, and fold in until fully incorporated.

Spoon the batter into the lined pan and smooth it over with a spatula. Bake for 30 to 35 minutes until the sponge springs back to the touch and an inserted skewer comes out clean. Let cool in the pan for about 5 minutes.

While the sponge pudding is baking, make the orange butterscotch sauce. Heat the superfine sugar in a medium pan over high heat and watch for it to melt. Keep swirling the pan (don't stir!) until it's fully melted and starting to turn golden. Wait for the caramel to go a deep amber color before slowly whisking in the heavy cream and orange juice. It might splutter a bit to start with—but don't be alarmed, just be careful. Add the salt, then slowly stir in the butter, a little at a time, until it's all mixed in.

Cut the still-warm sponge into large squares and serve smothered in the butterscotch sauce, adding a spoonful of crème fraîche, if desired.

# Chocolate Espresso Torte with Ginger Wine Pears

The opulent pairing of chocolate and pears is a classic—but add in coffee, ginger, and booze and you're ready for a party! This rich chocolate cake gives a second life to the coffee grounds left over in a cafetière or an espresso machine, and makes the torte all the more dark and delicious. We love serving it alongside these sweet poached pears, tender in texture but with a fiery kick of ginger.

SERVES 8

**For the torte**
6 ounces unsalted butter, softened, plus extra for greasing
2 teaspoons unsweetened cocoa powder, for dusting
7 ounces dark chocolate (70% cocoa solids)
1 ounce leftover coffee grounds (see tip)
4½ ounces superfine sugar
7 ounces ground almonds
1 teaspoon vanilla extract
¼ teaspoon fine salt
4 large eggs, separated

**For the pears**
14 ounces superfine sugar
20 fluid ounces ginger wine
1 teaspoon vanilla extract
2 cinnamon sticks
3 star anise
8 pears, slightly underripe, with stalks still intact

**For the topping**
3½ ounces dark chocolate (70% cocoa solids)
2 fluid ounces heavy cream

**To serve**
Crème fraîche

Preheat the oven to 300°F. Lightly grease the bottom and sides of a 10-inch springform cake pan with a little butter. Line the bottom with a circle of baking parchment and dust the inside edges of the pan with a little cocoa, tipping out any excess.

Break up the chocolate and place in a heatproof bowl. Melt it in the microwave in short bursts (stirring it regularly to avoid it burning). Alternatively, set the bowl over a pan of boiling water (ensuring the bottom of the bowl does not touch the water) until it's fully melted. Stir in the coffee grounds and set aside.

Using an electric mixer, cream together the butter and sugar until light and fluffy. Mix in the melted chocolate and coffee mixture, ground almonds, vanilla, salt, and egg yolks until well combined.

In a separate, clean bowl use a clean electric mixer to whisk the egg whites until they form stiff peaks when the beaters are lifted sharply out of the bowl. Gently fold the egg whites into the chocolate mixture until no whites remain, trying to retain as much air as possible.

Spoon the batter into the lined pan and smooth it out flat with a spatula. Bake for 35 to 40 minutes until the torte is firm on the edges but still a little squishy in the middle. Leave it in the pan to cool completely.

Meanwhile, poach the pears. Combine the sugar, ginger wine, vanilla, cinnamon, and star anise in a pan large enough that when the pears are added they can be fully submerged in the syrup. Set the pan over medium heat and bring to a boil, then reduce the heat and simmer for 5 minutes.

## TIP

If you haven't made a pot of coffee or have any used grounds on hand, you can use freshly ground coffee—just reduce the amount to ¾ ounce.

While the syrup is simmering, peel the pears, just removing the skin and keeping the stalks intact. Cut a very small slice off the bottom of each pear so they can stand upright on their bases.

Add the pears to the poaching liquid, bring back to a very gentle simmer, and cover with a lid. Cook for 20 to 30 minutes until tender when tested with an inserted toothpick or the point of a knife. Remove from the liquid with a slotted spoon and leave, standing upright, to cool. Set aside 3 tablespoons of the poaching liquid and save the rest for another use (see tip).

To make the topping, chop the chocolate as finely as you can and tip into a bowl. (If you have a food processor, it can make this a bit easier.) Heat the cream and 3 tablespoons of the poaching liquid in a small pan over medium heat until it starts to bubble. As soon as you see it bubble, immediately remove from the heat and pour the mixture over the chopped chocolate. Let stand for 1 minute before mixing it all together with a spatula until the mixture is thick and glossy.

Remove the torte from the pan and transfer it to a serving plate. Pour the topping mixture over the torte and spread it out with a spatula to create an even glaze that just starts to run down the edges.

Serve each slice of torte with a poached pear and a good spoonful of crème fraîche.

---

### TIP

Any leftover poaching syrup can also be refrigerated and used in cocktails—try adding a dash to some prosecco, or a G&T garnished with a slice of pear or lime. For a nonalcoholic cocktail, add 2 tablespoons of the syrup to a glass, top off with soda or tonic water, and garnish with a slice of pear or lime and a sprig of rosemary. Alternatively, the poaching liquid can be boiled down to a thick and sticky syrup that is delicious drizzled over ice cream, yogurt, waffles, pancakes, or oatmeal.

# Baked Cheesecake with Roasted Figs

Rachael is one of the unsung "boss babes" of the bakery, having carried us through some of our biggest challenges and changes. She's been steadfast and always championed others into the limelight. Her baked cheesecake, on the other hand, needs no introduction: gloriously silky and heaped with glistening honey-roasted figs, it'll unashamedly turn all the heads at the table.

SERVES 8 TO 10

For the base
3¼ ounces unsalted butter, melted, plus extra for greasing
7 ounces graham crackers
1 tablespoon superfine sugar

For the cheesecake filling
31¾ ounces cream cheese
3 tablespoons all-purpose flour
8 ounces superfine sugar
A pinch of fine salt
7 fluid ounces sour cream
2 teaspoons vanilla extract
3 extra-large eggs plus 1 yolk
Finely grated zest and juice of 1 lemon

For the topping
5 ounces sour cream
1 tablespoon superfine sugar
A squeeze of lemon juice

To decorate
4 fresh figs
1 tablespoon brown sugar
½ teaspoon ground cinnamon
2 tablespoons honey
2¼ ounces shelled pistachios and almonds, coarsely chopped

Preheat the oven to 325°F. Grease and line the bottom of a 9-inch round springform cake pan with baking parchment.

First, make the base. Put the graham crackers into a food processor and blitz to a fine crumb with no large lumps. Alternatively, put them into a sealable freezer bag and bash with a rolling pin.

Melt the butter in a pan over medium heat, then stir in the crumbs and tablespoon of superfine sugar. Once coated in the melted butter, tip the crumbs into the cake pan and press down to create a flat base layer. Bake for 10 minutes, then let cool.

Increase the oven temperature to 400°F.

Next, make the cheesecake filling. In a large bowl, beat the cream cheese for 2 to 3 minutes until loosened, then gradually beat in the flour, superfine sugar, and salt. Add the sour cream, vanilla extract, eggs and egg yolk, lemon zest, and juice and mix until smooth and uniform in consistency.

Grease the inside edge of the cake pan with a little more butter and pour the filling on top of the cracker base, smoothing it out with a spatula if it's not level. Bake for 15 minutes, then reduce the oven temperature to 195°F and bake for another 50 minutes until the cheesecake is firm around the edges with a little wobble in the middle. Turn off the oven and open the door, but leave the cheesecake in the oven for another 2 hours, to slowly cool down as the oven cools.

To make the topping, whisk together the sour cream with the superfine sugar and lemon juice. Once the cheesecake has cooled, spread the mixture over the top and transfer to the refrigerator to set for up to 8 hours or overnight.

At least 1 hour before serving, roast the figs. Preheat the oven to 350°F and slice each fig into quarters. Put the figs into a small roasting pan, sprinkle over the brown sugar and cinnamon, and bake for 15 to 20 minutes until softened and browned. Let cool for 15 minutes before drizzling over the honey.

Meanwhile, tip the chopped nuts onto a baking sheet and toast in the oven for 10 minutes until fragrant.

To serve, remove the cheesecake from the springform pan and transfer to a large plate. Place the roasted figs on top, drizzle with any remaining honey syrup from the figs, and sprinkle with the toasted nuts.

**TIP**

If you want to make this recipe gluten free, substitute gluten-free cookies for the graham crackers and use gluten-free all-purpose flour instead of regular all-purpose flour.

# Cinnamon-Swirl Bread-and-Butter Pudding

If you made our Cinnamon Swirls from earlier in the book (see page 52) and haven't managed to eat them all while they're still fresh (practically impossible in our bakeries), this recipe will transform your leftover buns into a wonderful, comforting, custardy dessert.

## SERVES 6 TO 8

¾ ounce unsalted butter, softened, for greasing

4 large (about 21 ounces), stale cinnamon buns

1¾ ounces raisins or golden raisins (chocolate chips are also delicious if you're not a fan of dried fruit)

4 large eggs

1 ounce dark brown sugar

1½ tablespoons dark rum

7 fluid ounces heavy cream

20 fluid ounces whole milk

2 teaspoons ground cinnamon

¼ teaspoon fine salt

2 tablespoons raw brown sugar

Lightly grease a 9 x 13-inch baking pan with butter.

Cut the stale cinnamon buns into vertical slices, ½ to ¾ inch thick. Arrange the slices, standing up and overlapping one another, in the dish. Sprinkle over the raisins, allowing some to drop in between the bun slices.

Whisk together the eggs, dark brown sugar, rum, cream, milk, cinnamon, and salt. Pour the mixture over the bun pieces and let stand for 30 minutes, so the bread can soak up the custard.

Meanwhile, preheat the oven to 340°F.

Sprinkle the raw brown sugar over the top of the pudding.

Bake for 40 to 45 minutes until it has puffed up and has a very slight wobble in the middle.

Let stand for 5 minutes before serving warm.

## KATIE'S

# Buttermilk Panna Cotta with Grapefruit Caramel

Utterly charming, just like Katie, these creamy panna cotta topped with glowing grapefruit caramel really are quite the picture. Katie's use of buttermilk is inspired by her Irish upbringing, and when it's made in small glasses with the distinct layers on show, no one can resist taking a spoon to this smooth and light cream.

MAKES 6 TO 8

For the panna cotta
3 sheets of leaf gelatin
12 fluid ounces buttermilk
    (or 10½ ounces yogurt
    and 1⅔ fluid ounces
    milk)
8½ fluid ounces heavy
    cream
1¾ ounces superfine sugar
Seeds from ½ vanilla bean

For the caramel
1¾ ounces superfine sugar
2½ tablespoons water
4 fluid ounces fresh red
    grapefruit juice
1 tablespoon salted butter

To serve
1 red grapefruit

For the panna cotta, first soak the gelatin leaves in a small bowl of cold water. Place 8½ fluid ounces of the buttermilk (or the 10½ ounces yogurt, if using) in a large heatproof bowl, along with the heavy cream and set aside.

Place the remaining 3½ fluid ounces of the buttermilk (or the whole milk, if using), the sugar, and the seeds from the vanilla bean in a small pan and bring to a boil.

Take the pan off the boil, squeeze any water out of the gelatin leaves, and add the gelatin to the pan, stirring until it is completely dissolved. Strain the mixture through a strainer into the bowl with the buttermilk and cream and stir until thoroughly combined.

Pour the mixture between 6 to 8 small serving glasses or ramekins (depending on their size), leaving about ¾ inch clear at the top. Place in the refrigerator to set for a minimum of 3 hours.

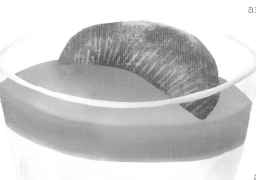

To make the caramel, put the sugar and water into a small pan and bring to a boil over medium heat. Cook until it becomes a dark amber color, then slowly add the grapefruit juice, a little at a time. Be careful—it will spit and spurt and the caramel will set hard in the pan. Bring the caramel back to a boil and simmer for about 5 minutes until the hardened sugar dissolves and it has reduced to a thicker, pourable sauce. Remove from the heat and stir in the butter, a little at a time, until it's all incorporated.

Transfer the warm caramel to a pitcher and leave at room temperature until the panna cotta are set.

To serve, slice the top and bottom off the grapefruit and, using even downward strokes, slice the skin off the grapefruit, making sure to remove any white pith. Cut in between the membranes to obtain whole segments. Squeeze any remaining grapefruit juice back over the segments. Spoon the caramel over the top of each panna cotta and place 1 to 2 grapefruit segments on top to decorate. Serve immediately.

# RACHEL'S
# Blueberry and Basil Pavlova

If you were to walk into our kitchen on week 21 of our training program, you would be met by a gaggle of trainees, excitedly huddled around mixers, in awe of what they'd just made for the first time: meringue. Thick and glossy, bright white peaks, whisked up from only a few egg whites and sugar—the wonder and thrill of it never gets old. Once the meringue is out of the oven and piled high with cream and fruit, our trainees' pride in their centerpiece creations quickly leads you to being handed platefuls of pavlova to try. This recipe is a favorite of Rachel, our bakery trainer and former head baker. We hope the enchanting combination of blueberries and basil in her compote fills your kitchen with the same wonder and joy as ours.

SERVES 8 TO 10

**For the meringue**
3 large egg whites
Finely grated zest of ½ lime
    plus 2 teaspoons lime juice
A pinch of fine salt
7 ounces superfine sugar
1 teaspoon cornstarch

**For the blueberry and basil compote**
14 ounces frozen blueberries
    (fresh are nice too)
2¾ ounces superfine sugar
2 teaspoons lime juice
1 tablespoon cornstarch
6 large fresh basil leaves,
    finely chopped

**To serve**
10 fluid ounces heavy cream
A handful of basil leaves
Finely grated zest of ½ lime

## TIPS
Make sure all the equipment you need is spotlessly clean and grease free.

A pavlova is best when baked and left to cool in the oven, the residual heat finishing the cooking. You can leave the oven door slightly ajar, if you wish, to avoid moisture buildup and help it dry out completely. We always bake the meringue the night before we want to serve it and let it cool as we sleep. All that's left to do on the day is to whip up some cream and compote and decorate your pav.

Preheat the oven to 350°F and line a baking sheet with baking parchment.

In a large clean bowl (see tip), use an electric mixer to whisk the egg whites, lime juice, and salt until they form stiff peaks when the beaters are lifted sharply out of the bowl. Whisk in the sugar, adding a third of it at a time and whisking for a couple of minutes between each addition. Once the meringue is really thick, whisk in the cornstarch. Finally, add the lime zest and gently fold it in.

Spoon the meringue into a heap on the lined baking sheet and gently spread to form an even 8-inch circle. Use your artistic freedom to make "waves" and small peaks in the meringue as desired.

Place in the oven and immediately reduce the temperature to 300°F. Bake for 1 hour until the outside is crisp, then turn the oven off and leave in the oven to cool completely (see tip).

To make the compote, tip the blueberries, sugar, and lime juice into a pan and let defrost over low heat for about 10 minutes, stirring every now and again. Turn the heat up to medium and cook down for about 10 minutes until some of the blueberries have burst.

In a cup or bowl, stir the cornstarch together with 2 tablespoons of cold water to a smooth paste. Add the paste to the blueberry pan, stir to thicken, and cook for a few minutes. Stir in the finely chopped basil, then remove from the heat and let cool completely— the compote will thicken further as it cools.

When the compote is completely cool, whip the heavy cream into soft peaks using an electric mixer—it's best to whip until the cream is almost thick and then stop and do the last bit by hand to avoid overwhipping and ending up with "crumbly" whipped cream. Take a large spoonful of the compote and gently fold it through the cream to ripple it with purple swirls.

Dollop the cream into a big pile in the center of the meringue and spread out almost to the edge. Spoon the remaining compote on top of the cream and spread it out, leaving some of the cream visible at the edge. Finish with a sprinkling of basil leaves and the lime zest.

# Amaretti Meringue Nests with Cherry Compote

For Erin

Grace originally came up with this stunning dessert after receiving an invitation to a dinner party. As someone who felt isolated from everyday relationships, Grace wanted to impress! Suffice to say, her crunchy amaretti cookie meringues filled with fresh cherry compote with its vivid pink coloring were a culinary game-changer. Not only did Grace's new friends enjoy her dessert, but it helped her find the courage to take a chance on life again. Grace decided to dedicate this recipe to Erin Pizzey*—a driving force for safety and friendship, opening up doors to people who are isolated. "She set a precedent that coincides with my journey. Without her, people like me may not have been helped!"

MAKES 6

For the meringue
2¾ ounces egg whites
    (from about 2 eggs)
¼ teaspoon almond extract
5¼ ounces superfine sugar
6 crunchy amaretti cookies,
    such as Amaretti di
    Saronno (3 ounces),
    plus an extra 2 cookies
    to decorate (see tip)

For the compote
5¼ ounces frozen cherries
1 ounce superfine sugar
2 tablespoons lemon juice

For the mascarpone cream
3½ ounces mascarpone
    cheese
1⅔ fluid ounces heavy
    cream
1 ounce confectioners' sugar,
    sifted
1 teaspoon vanilla extract

TIP
If you're making this as a gluten-free dessert, ensure you buy a brand of amaretti cookies that doesn't contain wheat.

*Erin Pizzey started the first domestic violence shelter in the modern world, in 1971.

Preheat the oven to 210°F and line a baking sheet with baking parchment.

In a spotlessly clean bowl, whip the egg whites, using an electric mixer on medium speed, until they have doubled in size and form stiff peaks when the whisk is lifted sharply out of the bowl. Turn the mixer to a higher speed and add the almond extract, then add the superfine sugar, a spoonful at a time, until the mixture is glossy and you can't feel any grains of sugar when it is rubbed between your fingers.

Crumble the amaretti cookies into 6 separate circles on the baking sheet. Carefully pipe or spoon the meringue mixture onto each cookie mound in a nest shape, making a dimple in the middle. Try to keep the cookie crumbs on the base of the meringue.

Bake the meringues in the oven for 2 hours, or until they lift off the baking parchment easily but before they have browned.

Meanwhile, make the compote. Place the cherries, superfine sugar, and lemon juice in a pan over low-medium heat and cook for 20 to 25 minutes, stirring occasionally, until the cherries have cooked down. Let cool.

To make the mascarpone cream, simply place the mascarpone in a bowl and beat it briefly to loosen. Add the heavy cream, confectioners' sugar, and vanilla, and whip until the mixture forms soft peaks—be careful not to overmix or it will become grainy.

Once the meringues and compote are cool and you are ready to serve, top each nest with some of the mascarpone cream, followed by a large spoonful of compote, letting it drip down the sides. Crumble over the remaining amaretti cookies and serve immediately (the meringues will go soggy if you do this in advance).

# INDEX

# SPECIAL INDEXES

## GLUTEN-FREE RECIPES

## LACTOSE-FREE RECIPES

## VEGAN RECIPES

## 30 MINUTES OR LESS RECIPES

## ECONOMICAL RECIPES

# ACKNOWLEDGMENTS

When it comes to thanking our ever-supportive and passionate community, the list could literally go on and on. Our journey has connected us with people who've traveled hundreds of miles to help us renovate, paint, and maintain our buildings; who have willingly volunteered to wash an endless array of pots; who have been inspired to paint, draw, and photograph our baked goods; who have used their influence to shed light on the work we do; who have sent encouraging words right when we needed them; and who donated clothes, food, and gifts for our wonderful women. You have helped us get to where we are and we thank you all deeply!

Firstly, thank you to the Kahaila community. This is where the idea for Luminary came about and we are so grateful to every single one of you who has journeyed with us through volunteering, continually praying for and championing this endeavor.

To Good Shepherd Mission Bethnal Green, our first home as a bakery. We thank you for taking a chance on us and believing in our vision. You not only made each and every one of us feel welcomed into your community, but you also supported our grassroots.

To Husk Coffee & Creative Space, thank you for being our home-in-transition. So many beautiful stories, memories, and adventures happened in your tiny kitchen and classroom. Thank you for making room for us to completely take over your cooking space when we needed to ramp up to full-time training and baking.

To all our dedicated stockists and customers, thank you for being the engine behind Luminary. For enabling us to employ more women who need a second chance.

Thank you to Ben & Jerry's and Food Innovation Solutions for taking a risk on us and partnering with our little social enterprise. You taught us so much about what it means to create such wonderful products.

Thank you to all our investors, donors, and financial supporters, for joining us on this exciting journey and for taking a chance on what we are doing. None of what we do could happen without you! Thank you for being there for us at whatever point you joined along the journey and for having faith in our desire to bring change.

Thank you to our selfless volunteers, mentors, and ambassadors, past and present, for being the heart and soul of Luminary. You went above and beyond to make us what we are today ... and helped us have so much fun along the way! A particular thank you to Rachel Joy Price, the creator of our iconic logo, for taking the time to form such a symbol of hope.

To our trustees and directors, you've brought in the support, wisdom, and guidance that we truly needed. Thank you for giving up your time, energy, and brains to steer this ship.

To the Duchess of Sussex and her wonderful team, thank you for sharing the work we are doing with the world, for taking the time to get to know us, and for championing our women so powerfully.

To Kate and her incredible team at HQ, to our creative copy editor, Emily, and to our clever designer, Georgie, thank you for your passionate care for our Luminary women and desire to do something so unique with this book. We are so grateful that you believed in us, encouraged us, and helped make it the best it could be.

To our talented illustrator, Carrie, thank you for working with us and introducing us to the beautiful world of watercolor. We are grateful for your dedication to helping bring our recipes to life.

To our dedicated literary agent, Charlotte, thank you for seeing something special in your local bakery. Others have asked us to create a book, but we felt so safe in your hands—thank you for everything you have done to make this a reality.

To all our fearless recipe testers around the world, thank you for your late-night escapades! All of the time and energy you put into making sure our recipes were delicious has been so valuable.

To the women who shared their stories in this book, thank you for opening up part of your life to us and the world. Your hope, transformation, and perseverance continue to inspire us all every day.

To all our trainees, past and present, thank you for being a part of our family and making it the fun, generous, supportive, empowering, diverse, beautiful thing that it is today!

To our devoted friends and family, thank you for being as much a part of the journey as everyone else. You have often been in the background, cheering us on, offering a listening ear, and giving us the energy we needed to keep going. You have been crucial in helping us continue to tackle barriers and grow our vision. Thank you for having our backs! And thank you again to all our recipe creators and contributors—your journey with us on this cookbook adventure has been a joy.

We are honored to have such a loyal community! We have seen ups and downs throughout the years as a social enterprise, but have risen above it more hopeful than before because of your devotion and faith in empowering all women. Together we have made, are making, and will continue to make a difference.

With love,
*Your Luminary Family*

# ABOUT LUMINARY

Luminary Bakery is a social enterprise supporting some of the UK's most disadvantaged women to thrive, through training, employment, and community.

This book includes contributions from many of the women in the Luminary community, carefully curated and written by our head bakery trainer **Rachel Stonehouse**. Rachel has worked closely with each contributor to ensure these recipes are delicious, creative, and easy for you to bake at home. Additional recipes are Luminary classics, and some she has created exclusively for this book. Rachel has been with Luminary since (almost) day one, moving to London in 2014 to join our fledgling bakery. She later took on the role of our head baker and now spends her days in Luminary's kitchen classroom, passing her baking skills onto the trainees on our Employability training programs.

Woven throughout this book are true stories from some of our incredible graduates, collated, and written by our communications officer, **Kaila H. Johnson**. Kaila had the honor of spending time interviewing these remarkable women and hearing the narratives and inspirations behind each of their recipe contributions. Having been a cheerleader of Luminary Bakery

from day one, Kaila has often been seen operating behind the scenes, helping fill the different positions that a budding charity and business need filling. She now spends her days writing and sharing with the world the stories of rising hope and the noticeable impact taking place at and through Luminary Bakery.

**Alice Williams**, founder of Luminary, wrote the introduction to *Rising Hope* and has worked closely with the writing team. Alice has led Luminary from the seed of an idea to the thriving multisite bakery it is today, with a dream of there being a Luminary Bakery wherever it is needed in the UK.

**Rachael Coulson**, Luminary's commercial director, has focused on the flow and composition of *Rising Hope*, shaping, and guiding its content to honestly reflect the true essence of Luminary and to captivate our readers with all the insight you would hope to gain from the first ever Luminary cookbook. Rachael joined Luminary three years ago, coming straight from the commercial world with a burning desire to use business as a force for change; she is excited to see how *Rising Hope* inspires others to enter the exciting and transformative world of social enterprise!

# RESOURCES

Luminary's social enterprise bakery is made up of talented bakers, baristas, and support workers offering opportunities for women to build a future for themselves. We provide a safe and professional environment, empowering women to build their careers through two years of training, community, and holistic support. During our 6-month Employability Training Program, we train groups of women covering baking skills to a professional standard, Level 2 Food Hygiene, and character development. Women also are given the opportunity to do work experience within Luminary's cafés and bakery production units. Following the training program and graduation, our women enter the 18-month Progression Support Program. They work one-on-one with our progression workers, have the opportunity to apply for paid work at Luminary or external employment opportunities, are linked up with a professional mentor to help reach their goals, are offered regular wellbeing workshops, and have access to ongoing practical support and signposting.

If you'd like to know more about Luminary Bakery, head to our website: **luminarybakery.com**

If you or somebody you know is affected by the issues raised in this book, you can find further information and resources at: **luminarybakery.com/resources**

Below are details for the enterprises started by our training program graduates, referenced in their stories:

Haliberry Cakes and Catering: haliberrycatering.co.uk

Bake Yourself Better: bakeyourselfbetter.com

Strength of a Woman: @strengthofawoman2019

First published in 2020 by HQ,
an imprint of HarperCollinsPublishers Ltd.

RISING HOPE.
Copyright © 2020 Luminary Bakery.

HarperCollins books may be purchased for educational, business,
or sales promotional use. For information please email the
Special Markets Department at SPsales@harpercollins.com.

Also published in 2020 by
Harper Design
*An Imprint of* HarperCollins*Publishers*
195 Broadway
New York, NY 10007
Tel: (212) 207-7000
Fax: (855) 746-6023
harperdesign@harpercollins.com
www.hc.com

Distributed in North America by
HarperCollinsPublishers
195 Broadway
New York, NY 10007

ISBN 978-0-06-304040-3

Library of Congress Control Number: 2020022431

Printed in Italy

First Printing, 2020

Illustration: Carrie May
Design: Georgina Hewitt
Project Editor: Emily Preece-Morrison
Commissioning Editor: Charlotte Mursell
Editorial Director: Kate Fox